"Father Bausch is a proven commodity as pastor, author, and storyteller. This collection of his homilies is excellent for devotional reading and as grist for the homiletic mill of busy pastors."

William C. Graham
National Catholic Reporter

"The author's refreshing approach to scripture could enrich the reader's private meditation. The humorous anecdotes sprinkled throughout might even be used to enliven one's daily conversations with others. As the author states, his stories are about 'people of grace' whose example will prod all of us to live more responsibly as followers of Christ."

Sr. Monica Zmolek, O.S.F.
The Catholic Sun

"If you have never heard a homily by Father Bausch, pastor of St. Mary's Church, Colts Neck, N.J., treat yourself to 35 of them by reading *Telling Stories, Compelling Stories*. The only thing missing here is the excellent delivery he brings to his homilies. But reading these stories is the next best thing to being there."

Patricia Yoczis
The Trenton Monitor

"The greatest challenge for the homilist is to deliver the message of scripture within a contemporary framework. Using real-life stories of people who have struggled, questioned, and come to grips with issues touching upon God and faith, the author has created a work that can be used effectively in liturgical or religious education settings."

E. Lazar
Liturgy

"Stories are remembered! ... ws the value of a compelling stor ... e use of story in these homilies. Valuable for homily preparation but also worthwhile for personal spiritual reading."

Patrick J. Riley
Emmanuel

"William J. Bausch has written a book of many stories 'to illuminate us with possibilities for life when we return to our ordinary world.' They invite us to personal responsibility, conversion, and 'quiet heroism.'"

Betty Puntel
The Living Light

"I strongly urge you to read Bausch's *Telling Stories, Compelling Stories: 35 Stories of People of Grace.* He uses flesh-and-blood characters who will challenge you in your daily life and guide you in seeking God's grace."

Henry Gosselin
Church World

"Father Bausch is a gifted homilist and storyteller. His book can be an inspiration to parish priests, but it can also be an inspiration for personal prayer. It would also work well with small discussion groups. If you can't have Bausch in your parish, at least have his words on your bookshelf."

Peggy Weber
Catholic Observer

"These homilies are exquisite studies in rhetorical understatement. Bausch knows exactly when to turn to an anecdote, quote scripture, introduce examples and characters, and invoke the moral of his story. And he knows when to cut the homiletics and let the story speak for itself."

Paul Matthew St. Pierre
British Columbia Catholic

"Preachers looking for anecdotes, scriptural links to modern personalities and events, and conversational delivery will find Bausch's *Telling Stories, Compelling Stories* a handy tool. A list of the Scriptures (from the three lectionary cycles) on which the homilies are based appears at the end of the book for quick reference."

Church Magazine

WILLIAM J. BAUSCH

TELLING
STORIES
COMPELLING
STORIES
35
Stories
of People
of Grace

TWENTY-THIRD PUBLICATIONS
Mystic, CT 06355

Fifth printing 1996

Twenty-Third Publications
185 Willow Street
P.O. Box 180
Mystic, CT 06355
(860) 536-2611
800-321-0411

ISBN 0-89622-456-2
Library of Congress Catalog Card Number 90-71137
Printed in the U.S.A.

Preface

Telling Stories, Compelling Stories is essentially about people of grace, a theme closely related to the Catholic sense of incarnation. As Louis Cameli wrote:

> Narrative theology has alerted us to the plot of redeeming love which God weaves in the story of our lives. Narrative understandings of faith also restrain us from identifying faith with a generalized philosophy of life. The narrative approach to faith confronts us squarely with the scandalous particularity of the Incarnation, the utter uniqueness of the Word made flesh in time and space, and then the challenge of the particularity of our own lives as the place of God's transforming love [*Church* (Spring 1990)].

The people in these homilies—from Mrs. Kendal, a British actress who performed mostly in the last century, to Glenn Cunningham, an Olympic champion runner of this century—all translate grace into flesh and blood, all reflect an aspect of the gospel at hand, and all give us models of possibilities in our own lives. So you'll find many stories about many people in these homilies, stories, I hope, not merely cute or homey—a pitfall about which Cameli warns—but, as Andrew Greeley expresses it, intriguing and teasing stories about real people which invite us into the story's own world "to illuminate us with possibilities for life when we return to our ordinary world."

The stories have been gleaned from so many sources in general reading that I hardly know where I first read or heard them. I just know that when I did, they caught me as possibilities and I clipped them out and stored them in a three-ring binder to be used as the spirit might suggest. Many of these stories and sometimes even the line of development have been suggested by several of the fine homily help-services to which I subscribe. If the people who put these out ever wonder if they help, let me gratefully express the opinion that they do. Such helps are modest in that they claim merely to suggest a train of thought or an outline, point to some stories, and offer all those elements to us homilists, not so that we might slavishly copy them, but rather so that we might use our own imaginations and life experiences to marry them into a coherent message for our people and our time in the light of what's happening today. If any of those who work on such help-services read this book, I hope they will recognize a narrative or a line of development suggested by them and brought to a new form in some of these homilies.

But I've used a few sources more directly, which I wish to acknowledge here. The notions of avarice and sloth in the homily "Capital Sins" come from Monica Furlong's *Christian Uncertainties* (Cambridge, Mass.: Cowley, 1975); some of the thoughts in "Holy Thursday" come from Don Aycook's book *Eight Days That Changed the World* (Nashville: Broadman Press, 1990); some of the thoughts and expressions in "Easter" come from an interview given by William Willimon (see *Leadership* [Spring 1990]); the story "How Death Became Life" in "Entering Passiontide" is from Catherine de Hueck Doherty (*Not Without Parables*, Notre Dame, Ind.: Ave Maria Press, 1977), and the images found in "Images for the End of Summer" can be found in Leo Holland's *Images of God* (Notre Dame, Ind.: Ave Maria Press, 1984).

Most people will read these homilies piecemeal; that is wise because here and there some themes overlap and recur, and it's good to remember that these homilies were given with months and sometimes years between them. And, as might be expected, there is bound to be some unevenness of quality and appeal among thirty-five such homilies. If there is any over-arching premise behind these homilies and the stories they contain about people of grace, it is that of responsibility. There is a reaction setting in against the popular cultural conviction that we are a "no-fault" tribe, helpless victims of the environment or faulty genes. Cognitive therapy and the success of the twelve steps of AA in its many forms are helping us reclaim some measure of responsibility for the direction of our lives and of this world. In Christian terms, by the grace of God we can repent and move into renewed lives; we can make a difference; we do not have to be passive in the face of what seems at times overwhelming evil; there are things we can do, gestures we can make, decisions we can implement, all forms of quiet heroism of which the individual is capable. The people of grace in these homilies both demonstrate these truths and encourage us to do likewise.

I wish to thank Dot Boese and Jerry DiSalvo for recording these homilies, Gloria Ziemienski for transcribing them, and the people who first heard them and did not complain. At least not openly.

For Kelly, Arrow, and Beau squared

Qui me amat, amet et canem meum
St. Bernard

Contents

Telling Stories,
Compelling Stories

1

✝

Be Open

Mark 7:31–37

When I was reflecting on this gospel I was trying to enter into the story of the principal figure, the man who needed help, the man for whom it was said, "Be open."

I tried to imagine what it must be like to be deaf, not to hear all the sounds we take for granted. In addition, this man had some speech impediment. So he could neither hear nor speak. What must it be like to be imprisoned like that? How do such people survive? Do they ever get free? The search for answers led me to consider three people and how, through them, God touched others and freed them—and, therefore, how God frees us. You may recognize one or two of these people.

The first person takes us back to June 27, 1880, in Tuscumbia, Alabama. There a delightful, darling little girl was born, healthy and well. But she soon picked up some kind of fever of undisclosed origin, and before she was a year and a half, she could not hear and she could not see. She was now both deaf and blind. She could relate to this gospel story very poignantly.

This girl, of course, was Helen Keller. Her family, as you know, if you read her story or saw the play or movie *The Mira-*

cle Worker, overcompensated for her handicap by spoiling her so rotten that she became an uncontrolled, uncontrollable hellion of a child. Later on she tried to describe this period of her life when she was like the man in the gospel, what it was like to be imprisoned in her body, not hearing or seeing. At one point she likened her condition to a ship that was in a dense fog with no compass, no plumb line, no nothing. She waited like that ship in the fog, she said, fighting back anger and rage, being overcome by the enormity of the obstacles she knew she faced. She waited and waited until March 3, 1887, the day when the fog began to lift.

So I went back to her autobiography and I fished out one or two paragraphs that described her waiting. She wrote:

> The most important day I remember in all my life is the one in which my teacher, Annie Mansfield Sullivan, came to me. I am filled with wonder when I consider the immeasurable contrast between the two lives which it connects.
>
> On the afternoon of that eventful day I stood on the porch, dumb and expectant. I guessed vaguely from my mother's signs and from the hurrying to and fro that something unusual was about to happen. So I went to the door and I waited on the steps. The afternoon sun penetrated the mass of honeysuckle that covered the porch and fell on my upturned face. My fingers lingered almost unconsciously on the familiar leaves and blossoms which had just come forth. I did not know what the future held, of marvel or surprise for me. Anger and bitterness had preyed upon me continually, and left me with a great struggle. I felt approaching footsteps. I stretched out my hand as I supposed it to be my mother. But someone took it, and I was caught up and held close in the arms of someone who had come to reveal all things to me. And more than all else, to love me.

If you remember the play or movie, this Annie Sullivan did

give the child enormous love, but she also gave her firm and, at times, violent discipline. This was a little wild animal of a child and Annie's combination of very tender and warm love and very stern and uncompromising discipline—her demand for obedience—touched this girl deeply and made her into a human being and a very great one at that. Even such—at times—a bitter and cynical soul as Mark Twain, who got to know Helen Keller, reckoned her and Napoleon as the two most interesting figures in the nineteenth century. Napoleon because he had conquered the world in his quest for power, and Helen Keller because she had conquered her own physical limitations to become a beautiful and noble lady.

The second name you may not know as well, but another era knew Mrs. Kendal as a famous British actress. She was portrayed in the movie and play *The Elephant Man*—that story of a man so called because of his excruciatingly horrible deformity. There is in the play a particular incident that I recall. As the actress went to see the elephant man and she held out her hand to shake his, he brought forth the less deformed of his two hands. Mrs. Kendal stood there and looked him in the eye and shook her head—indicating that that was not sufficient. The elephant man hesitated for a long time and finally, after a pause of about ten minutes, out from under his coat he brought his more horribly disfigured and deformed hand, and Mrs. Kendal took *that* hand in hers and smiled. And just before the curtain drops on the first act, the elephant man remarks that "that is the first time I'd ever held a woman's hand"; and much of the spiritual healing that occurs in his life came from that touch.

The third figure is anonymous. He's a man whose action I witnessed in an office building in New York, one of those huge skyscrapers of a building. A man, like a few hundred others, was there with his stereotypic briefcase and was running to the bank of elevators so that he could get to whatever office he was headed for. As he was going by, there was a woman standing there with a little boy. As he passed, he adroitly skirted around them, but he paused just long enough to lay his hand—quite lovingly—on the child's head and tousle his hair. And then he caught his elevator.

I reflected later that what I had witnessed says that no matter what kind of structures we put up, no matter how artificial our lives become, even in the concrete jungle there is something about a little child that resonates within us all. And in the hustle and bustle of it all, this man took time to touch a child. Maybe he reminded him of his own child; maybe it was the one human touch of his day before he sat before his computers and machines. Maybe his action was a simple touch-base with humanity.

Looking at this from the child's point of view, I wondered what he thought about it. He just saw the back of a man leaving, but someone had touched him with obvious care and obvious love and it was a reaffirming kind of touch; in an often mad world that catalogs nightly the number of accidents, murders, rapes, and hurts, it was a touch that said, "I love you and I'm concerned about you."

When I thought about these three people in relationship to this gospel, trying to relate to this man who could neither talk nor hear, I thought to myself, "But isn't that the way God touches us when we are blind, deaf, and dumb in a numbing world?" I mean, God touches us in the same three ways. At times God touches us as Annie Sullivan touched Helen Keller: violently and with demands. These are the people who have had violence in their lives—an accident, a death, a sudden trauma that just tore their lives apart—yet they have the opportunity to grow and become better for it all, to answer a new and different call.

I think of St. Paul literally being struck off his horse. I think of St. Augustine's depression. I think of Ignatius shot in the leg. I think of the young widow Elizabeth Ann Seton alone in New York with relatives who didn't like her, bereaved and with a flock of kids crying on the streets, and saying to herself, "What am I going to do with my life?" So God comes like Annie Sullivan, comes with demands, comes asking obedience to God's rules, life, and fierce love.

Second, God comes like Mrs. Kendal. God looks at our deformities. We hide them from each other and we hide them from ourselves. Underneath our cloaks we have our sins and things we would not like anyone else to know about us. Habits and addictions and maybe things in our past that are very, very heavy. But God comes like Mrs. Kendal and, of course, we treat him like we treat others. We offer God our least horrible side and try to fool even God. And God stands there like Mrs. Kendal and waits. God will not have our public side nor will he have our sanitized side. He asks for our most unseemly side, he asks for our most shameful sin. He asks for our deepest weakness, and will not be content until, out of the darkness, we present these to him. And with kindness God grasps our sin and weakness in his hand, and the healing begins. God comes to us that way if we but knew it.

And finally I suggest that God comes to us gently and with affection; that in the hustle and bustle of life—as we're moving down the fast lane and as we wonder where the days go and what's happening in our lives and we're running for the car, the bus, the train, the plane, running the kids here and there— we realize that somewhere there was a gentle touch that day. And the touch was God's.

So the gospel speaks to us in our imprisonment, speaks to us in our sometimes deafness and inability to speak or see, and I think the gospel message says: if we would but be attuned in prayer and contemplation we would recognize that God in fact does enter our lives. As we move about in our various imprisonments, if we would just be still, we would feel the hand of the Lord: sometimes demanding, sometimes healing, and sometimes affirming—but there.

So the gospel is not a story, I would suggest, from the past. It is a statement and paradigm of the present. It just takes, I think, a little listening, a little sensitivity, and a little quiet to recognize God—the God who shakes us like Annie Sullivan, the God who wants our ugliness like Mrs. Kendal, the God who affirms like the anonymous man.

"Be open," said Jesus. Be open to the time of his visitation.

2

Ananias: The Missing Ingredient

Acts 9:1–20

During this week, I was led to think of several people: Charles Bronson, Bernhard Goetz, Harrison Ford, and this little man named Ananias.

And the reason I thought of them is because all of us are caught up in the Libyan raid, the acts of terror, and our country's retaliation.[1] And perhaps it is right that we resonate with this act of retaliation—when people go around killing our fellow citizens, then sooner or later, when diplomacy fails, one has to take action. A sign that this retaliation has struck a chord in us is that about 70 percent of the American people approve of what the president has done.

It's the same kind of support that Bernhard Goetz got when he shot those kids in the subway.[2] How much harassment and

---

1 In April 1986, U.S. forces bombed targets in Libya in retaliation for Libyan-backed acts of terrorism against U.S. citizens. One of the targets was the residence of Muammar el-Qaddafi, the Libyan leader believed to be behind the terrorist acts.
2 On December 22, 1984, a group of youths approached Bernhard Goetz on a New York subway train. Having been mugged before, Goetz feared what the youths would do and opened fire on them.

terror can a person take? And Charles Bronson's films about revenge and retaliation are very popular for that same reason. People finally get to a frustration point and say, "We do not like to live as hunted people." And the urge is to retaliate. And those of you who saw *Witness* with Harrison Ford—remember when he was hanging out in disguise as one of the Amish, who are peace-loving people? You remember that particular scene in town when the young hoodlums started to mock the Amish, and rubbed an ice-cream cone on one of them. He was a big, strapping guy. But they were taking advantage of his pacifism, and we felt the indignity of it, as also, I suspect, we felt the glee when Harrison Ford got out *(he* was not Amish, but a Philadelphia cop in disguise) and creamed the two kids, breaking the nose of one of them, saying that's what they deserved for harassing decent people.

You see the same kind of thing in the scripture passage before us. There's this man named Saul, and what he is doing is pretty much the same thing as what these other bullies and terrorists have done, and he is doing it legally. He has gotten letters from Damascus giving him permission to ferret out men, women, and children who belong to this new Christian way, and to throw them in prison, perhaps even to be killed. This is the same Saul, by the way, whose hands are still red from the blood of the first martyr, Stephen. He too deserves retaliation.

So all up and down the line, I think we can resonate with this, and uneasy as we might be, we feel that sooner or later someone has to deal with subway thieves, street hoodlums, and fanatic terrorists who harm innocent people.

But there's another part to this impulse to retaliate and as you read further in today's scripture you discover a little man named Ananias. And Ananias has a vision in which the Lord tells him to go to Straight Street in Damascus and to baptize Saul. And Ananias says very sensibly and very critically, "No way. Do you know what you're asking me to do? This is the man who's running around throwing people in jail, taking part in murder. He is one bad number. He is the Qaddafi of the day."

But the Lord comes back to Ananias and says, "You do what

I tell you because there has been a conversion here of this evil and wicked man, and he's going to be my disciple to the gentile world."

And so with fear and trepidation Ananias sets off. You can imagine how he felt before he knocked on the door—wondering whether he would get karated to death, or what. Or wind up in jail, or dead himself.

I think there's a point to the story that we who believe in the gospel have to come to terms with, and that is this. While we are rightly upset with terrorism, while all civilized people shudder at their safety, there's a dimension that we're called to that has nothing to do with pacifism, but has everything to do with the gospel. And that is that we are not allowed to cut off the Spirit. And by that I mean that Ananias was not permitted to write off Saul as a murderous villain because the possibility of the Spirit to change that man's heart was always there. He was to open the door, even to murderous Saul.

So the point for us is this: to challenge our Christian conscience. With all of the reaction that we understandably feel against Qaddafi, whether we feel it was too bad he didn't get killed or whatever, has any one of us prayed for him? Not easy to do, not comfortable to do, but that's beside the point. We have a right to our feelings of wanting revenge and retaliation, but that's beside the point. The point for believers who gather around the eucharist and around Jesus who cried from the cross, "Father, forgive them," is at least to pray for this hateful person so as not to confine God, who has the power to turn a heart of stone to a heart of flesh.

Suppose, for example, that Ananias had not prayed for Saul. Would we have St. Paul? I think of Dorothy Day, in her early years, as an unwed mother and as a card-carrying communist. Suppose no one had opened the door so she could begin to develop into the beautiful saint that she became. I think of Thomas Merton. Agnostic, atheist, living the high life up there in Greenwich Village, fathering a child out of wedlock. Suppose no one had opened the door for him? I think of that Watergate scoundrel, Charles Colson. Suppose no one had opened the door for him so that he could become the born-again Christian that he is now. I think of St. Augustine, who certainly led a terrible, evil life. Suppose his mother, Monica, had never said a prayer for him because he was beyond reprieve, and beyond redemption. Christianity would have been entirely different without him.

So I guess what I'm saying here is that we Christians always have to come to terms with the hard parts of the gospel. I'm not saying that we have to take terrorism lying down, or that we should disapprove of what President Reagan did. All this is beside the issue I'm trying to share, and that is this: Have we prayed for Qaddafi? Sounds ridiculous to say it, but we are ridiculous Christians. Somewhere along in the week, did we pray for this evil, wicked man? If we did not, then it means that we foreclosed on God's Spirit, and we probably would not have prayed for Augustine or Merton, or Dorothy Day or Charles Colson, or anybody else who did a complete turnabout in their evil lives. If we did not, we foreclosed on the Spirit. If we did not, then somewhere along the line we were not as Christian as we thought we should be. We're entitled to our feelings, but we're also entitled, as believers, to pray for the wicked, that they may be converted.

So we think this over. Maybe today we might offer a silent prayer for this man. Certainly he is wicked. Certainly he promotes murder and terror. Certainly he's unworthy, and maybe he's mad, but Magdalene was no prize, and Peter was no saint when the Lord met him. And if Jesus came to save only the saved, none of us would be open to his grace.

So we're simply asked to put on the mind of Christ, as the convert, Saul, would write later on. And this doesn't stop with us—it has also to do with our children. I think this is important because I fear sometimes for our children; we and our children hear people say that Qaddafi should be "wasted," to use that terribly vulgar term that reduces people to objects. You see all kinds of signs in the paper, all kinds of vile and wicked and vulgar and obscene talk about Qaddafi. And I say, "Okay, you can have that." But if that's all you and your children react to, we're not training them as Christians. And after they have gone through all that stuff that they see in the media, on television, and have heard all the obscenities and all the things that should be done to this rotten person, have we challenged our children and our teenagers to pray for him? Do we believe in the power of prayer? Do we believe in the Spirit? Do we believe in conversion? Do we believe in the Jesus who prayed for his people who were in the process of unjustly murdering him? Do we say something like that to the kids when they're talking about "that nut Qaddafi," about "wasting" him, about sending him a bomb, and about doing all kinds of other things? When they've said those things, do you add the Christian dimension? At grace before meals, or at night prayers, why don't you pray for him? Because I'm convinced that in the long run, it is people who will pray for their enemies who will make more of a difference than those who merely, and only, strike back. And I think it is an attitude that has to be cultivated in our families and in our children, otherwise we become part of the problem. And to become as vile and hateful as Qaddafi, is to give him victory over our souls as well as our bodies.

So we are called to be like little Ananias. And maybe he might be our patron saint for this week of terrible news, and terrorist attacks, and reprisals. And maybe little Ananias is the one we have to imitate, the one who first said, "Lord, he's a nut, he's a killer, he's vile, he's wicked."

But the Lord said, "He doesn't know it yet, but he's going to be a great apostle, and I will show how much he will endure for my name's sake."

At least that was a beginning. Paul could have rejected Ananias, but that's beside the point. The point is God. The point is grace. The point is gospel. The point is Ananias. The point is ourselves.

3

✝

Bartimaeus

Mark 10:46–52

If we are not blind it is most difficult for us to imagine what it must mean to be that way day after day, year after year. We can get some inkling from Sheila Hock. She is a British house-wife who for thirty long years had not been able to see. Then she was operated on.

She was in the hospital when her bandages came off. She had never seen before and suddenly she saw. She explained later: "It was like an electric shock, as if something hit me." She had gotten a plate full of food, the first meal she ever saw, and she said, "I thought it would be easy to eat because I could see what I was doing. I would aim my fork for a piece of toma-to and miss it." She had to close her eyes to be able to eat that first meal.

She went into the street to go home, and she said, "I looked at the pavement and it was moving and the lampposts and the trees were moving so fast that I wanted to shout *stop!*" Then she added, "I never knew the world was so beautiful. I had a picture in my mind of what I thought my husband looked like because I had felt his features, but he was a lot better looking than I thought and I was pleased about it."

Things like that, I imagine, must have happened to that man Bartimaeus at the moment that he saw.

To be able suddenly to see must be a terrific experience. Very many people, even today, have that kind of experience in a spiritual way. I mean, they suddenly "see." They see all. They can't stop talking about it. They say that they see Jesus as their personal savior, that they are born again, and they write books and pamphlets with titles like "Suddenly I Saw," meaning they accepted the Lord Jesus Christ.

Your response to all this might be, "Good for them. Good for Sheila Hock. Good for Bartimaeus. I envy them. But me? Me, to tell the truth, I have a different experience. I feel like I'm still sitting in the dark and crying out:

"Jesus, son of David, have pity on me. I begin to clean the house and before I'm half finished the dust is beginning to settle again. What's the use? I prepare a meal and while I'm doing it, I'm thinking of a menu for the next meal. And the cycle continues and no one cares. I was considered important when I was raising the children, but they're on their own now. Oh, I know they love me, but the fact is they have gone and they don't call me or visit me that much. I work and my husband works, but we don't seem to go anywhere. I feel useless and I don't see anything down the road. I'm a blind beggar.

"Jesus, son of David, have pity on me. I go to work and the system is doing things I don't like. I disagree with the dog-eat-dog attitude and the ruthless methods that are used, but I feel stuck, powerless. My opinions don't seem to count; my job, like anybody's today, is not really secure. I'm too old to start somewhere else again and too young to retire. I have to protect my pension and my family's security. I take my paycheck and I go sit by the side of the road and don't see anything down it. I'm a blind beggar.

"Jesus, son of David, have pity on me. I spend most of my

time in a senior citizen's apartment. The children don't call very often. I'm no longer able to work, no longer able to contribute. I feel useless and don't see anything down the road. I'm a blind beggar.

"Jesus, son of David, have pity on me. Our marriage is falling apart. He won't go for counseling. We don't believe in divorce and the children need us. But it's a dead end. I dread the years ahead of just coping, arguing, distancing, dying. I can't see any solution down the road. I'm a blind beggar."

But our gospel writer, Mark, had precisely such people in mind when he left us, in the story of Bartimaeus the beggar, a four-part plan, if you will, about what brought about his cure and what might bring about ours as we too cry out, "Jesus, son of David, have pity on us."

First, in Mark's story, Bartimaeus hears about Jesus and calls out to him. So too for all of us blind people. The first step to seeing is prayer, calling upon the Lord mightily.

Second, Bartimaeus is rebuked. But he pays no attention. On the contrary, he cries out all the louder. We too are often rebuked, harshly or kiddingly, often by well-meaning people: "What you need is a good psychiatrist....Forget it, you don't have it....Religion is obsolete in this day and age....Everybody's doing it....You're wasting your time....Do you think God cares about you? God has other things to care about." We too must persevere in calling on the Lord. We must cry out all the louder.

Third, blind Bartimaeus is told to come to Jesus. He hesitates, but finally he casts aside his cloak and goes in the dark. Why did he hesitate? To answer that we must remember the significance of his cloak. It was his mat, his bed, his warmth, his security blanket. And his one possession. To let go of it was to let go of all he depended on. And that's exactly what Mark is saying. Let go of what you think is so critical and important and necessary and risk all to run to Jesus. If you cling to your self-made security, like Magdalene clinging to the feet of Jesus, the Spirit cannot come. Let go of the securities, the defenses, the devices the world recommends. Gaining is in the losing.

Once upon a time there was an old man from the lovely

island of Crete. He loved his land with a deep intensity, so much so that when he knew he was about to die he had his sons bring him outside and lay him on the ground. As he was about to expire he reached down by his side and clutched some earth in his hands. He died a happy man.

He now appeared before heaven's gates. God, in the guise of an old, white-bearded man, came out to greet him. "Welcome," he said, "you've been a good man. Please come into the joys of heaven." But as the man was about to enter through the pearly gates God said, "Please, you must let the soil go." "Never!" cried the old man, stepping back. "Never!" And so God sadly departed, leaving the old man outside the pearly gates. A few eons went by and God came out again, this time in the guise of an old friend, an old drinking crony. They had a few drinks, told some stories, and then God said, "All right, time to enter heaven, friend. Let's go." And they started for the pearly gates. And once more God requested that the old man let go of his soil, and once more the old man refused.

More eons rolled by. God came out once more, this time in the guise of the old man's delightful and playful granddaughter. "Oh, granddaddy," she said, "you're so wonderful and we all miss you. Please come inside with me." The old man nodded as she helped him up, for by this time he had grown very old indeed and very arthritic. In fact, so arthritic was he that he had to prop up the right hand holding Crete's soil with his left hand. They moved toward the pearly gates, and at this point his strength quite gave out. His gnarled fingers would no longer stay clenched, with the result that the soil sifted out between them until his hand was empty. Empty-handed, he entered heaven. The first thing he saw was his beloved island.

Bartimaeus, who let go and saw, would appreciate that story.

Finally, Mark lets us know that Bartimaeus is a beggar with no resources of his own, no gift to give in return. The only thing he has to present to Jesus is his need. Mark suggests that maybe that's just the way we must be. Stop bargaining with Jesus. Just offer him our need. No bribes, no false promises, no silly vows, just our emptiness, our need.

Not a bad plan for those who want to see God: prayer and more prayer; perseverance even when rebuked; letting go to let God in, as they say; and humility. A good gospel to digest.

Before we close, something else in this gospel nags as a parting shot. You can't help feeling that there's something more between the lines here. Mark seems to be suggesting that Bartimaeus was cured precisely because, although blind in the physical sense, he was better able to see than those with two good eyes. His humility entitled him to a cure. You get this subliminal message because in Mark 10:35–45, the passage that precedes the one at hand, Mark has Jesus' disciples failing to really see him as they maneuver and jockey for positions at Jesus' right and left hand. And Mark has Jesus ask of his disciples the very same question he asked of Bartimaeus, "What do you want?" James and John wanted power and so failed to see. Bartimaeus wanted Jesus, and so he did see.

4

+

The Prodigal Son

Luke 15:11–32

We have heard this parable of the prodigal son a few zillion times. It's probably the most famous of all the parables of Christ and one of the most famous stories in the world. So after having heard it all the years we've been coming to church, is there anything new or different to say about it?

Well, I would like to take the parable and, like one does with a diamond, turn it around three ways to see what freshness it has to offer, what telling nuances are hidden there that might nourish us.

For a first look notice this: the father divides his estate openly, so that before he dies his sons know exactly what's coming to them. The father doesn't have to do this. It's really a foolish thing to do, to reveal his assets so fully, to be so transparent. So the point being made is that the father is exceedingly generous and open. But his act also sets up his sons, now knowing what they can expect, to wish that he would soon die. The elder son really seems not to care about any of this. He can wait. But the younger son cannot: "Give me my inheritance now. I can't wait around for you to die." And implicit in that is the wish that in fact his father would die. From any son, much less the younger son, to imply this to his father is a grave insult, one which this father seems to absorb.

In the course of the story the younger son, who is in a far-off country, is sent to feed the swine. You have to remember that this is a Hebrew boy. Pork is unclean, forbidden. To tend the swine is equivalent to becoming alienated from his tradition, his custom, his values. And so, the moment the son agrees to do that, at that moment he knows himself to be an outcast from his people, from his father's house. All the more poignant and marvelous is it therefore that when his son returns as an outcast and renegade, the father runs to accept him still as a son, not as an alien traitor. That's a detail we should not overlook.

Another interesting detail is that the elder son refuses to enter the house. In that Middle East tradition this is the greatest of insults. The father has every right to bristle and banish this elder son for refusing to enter the ancestral home. But he doesn't. Once more he takes the initiative. He himself goes out to this son also and tries to win him over. Note that in every situation of insult—the unspoken wish that he would die, the son who sold the father's tradition down the river, and the refusal of the other son to come inside the house—the father advances and invites beyond the insult. What a revelation Jesus is making of what God is like!

Let's now turn the story around another way. Realize what is really being said down deep. The younger son does not want a father. The older son does not want a brother. And right there we have society's besetting sins. There are people who want no father, no one to answer to, no limit, no restraint, no relationship, no responsibility, no judgment. They wish their father, God, dead. They want to be free to do their own destructive thing. The nightly newscasts are full of them and their sound and fury.

Then there are those who say, "I have no brother. I have no concern. No one has a claim on me." Racism and discrimination and bias are "natural" to such people. The corporal and spiritual works of mercy make no sense to these people. Make it fast, make it big. It's the survival of Number One that counts.

And there is one final facet as we turn this story around one more time. Usually we consider three people in this story: there's the younger son, there's the older son, and there's the father. But there is one more hidden character who may be the most sinister of all. He is the crafty and cunning man who offered the job of tending the swine to the younger son. Remember once more, this is a Hebrew lad. He is up against it. No money, no friends. He is down and out. A stranger in a strange place. You can almost see this man smiling as he says, "O.K. Hebrew boy, it's the pigs or nothing!" In short, this wicked man took advantage of the boy's plight and vulnerability to alienate him from his people, from his culture, from his childhood values, from his heritage. Do we have people like that? Every day.

In any large city you will find smiling people at the bus stations stalking the runaway adolescents who get off, knowing that very soon they will be desperate for food, clothing, and shelter. And they will say, "O.K. boy, O.K. girl, sell us your body and we'll give you something to eat. Sell your heritage, your culture, your religion, your values, all that you have been taught." Soliciting for the pigsty happens every day.

It happens on television as the moral values of honesty, decency, pacifism, and chastity are sold down the river to sensationalism, the quick deal, violence, and free-wheeling sex. It happens as the lure of materialism entices parents to the good life at the expense of their marriages, children, and friendships. It happens when a big-time sport tempts the highschooler to a share in its ten-billion-dollar market. It happens whenever anyone sells your child a drink or a snort of cocaine. Like the man in our story, there are lots of people waiting to take advantage of our vulnerabilities, asking for our heritage in exchange for a momentary high.

I just read of one such person in our local paper. I was saddened to read a story of a forty-three-year-old man whom I knew as a youngster in another parish, Ritchie Johnson. He made a video, the paper said. The video was made for kids and urged them to keep away from the drugs he couldn't resist. He says on that video, "I started using alcohol when I was about thirteen or fourteen because of peer pressure." The buyer of one's birthright doesn't have to be an adult. Someone asked him to sell his heritage just to be "in." Ritchie continues, "Because of my friends I started drinking. I couldn't stop there. Under the influence of alcohol I started doing speed and pot and various things. I fell in love with getting high. I thought it was the greatest thing that ever happened to me. And little did I know—little did I know—that I'd be sentenced, that I'd spend one-third of my life in prison for drugs."

The reason Ritchie made this video was because he was dying of AIDS. He got it from one of the needles. So before he died he wanted to tell kids that when the pusher comes along asking for their heritage in exchange for a high, "Don't do what I did." The story of Ritchie ends sadly. The paper says that he was found dead in a local railroad yard. He was hardly recognizable except for the marks on his body where he had been shooting up all his life.

As the gospel suggests—no, pleadingly invites—run away from those shadowy figures and return to your father's house. Why? Because there's somebody there to hug and kiss you, someone unlike any other father in the world, someone who can absorb all of your insults and hurts and rejections and sins, someone who, in spite of it all, will call for a celebration and throw a party. This is a "good news" gospel, a burst of mercy, forgiveness, and reconciliation.

Coincidentally enough, I heard this story in modern form the other day, and I'd like to end with it. It was told to me by a youth minister and friend of mine named Tony, who's from another diocese. He was preparing to give a retreat for the kids and he couldn't get his thoughts together. So it was about two o'clock in the morning and he said, "I've just got to have a break here." So he went down to the local diner to get a cup of coffee. While he was sitting there at the counter three guys came in—three bums, as he called them, down-and-outers—and one of them said to the others in a kind of half-drunk voice, "Tomorrow's my birthday." One of the other guys said, "So what?" And they had a cup of coffee and left.

After they left, Tony said to the waiter, "These guys come in here all the time?" The waiter answered, "Yeah, they come in here every night around two o'clock. They have some kind of crummy watchman's job at the factory." So Tony said to the waiter, "I overheard the guy say it's his birthday. What do you say? He'll be here around two o'clock tomorrow morning—let's throw him a party." "Eh," said the waiter, "why not?"

So Tony got some decorations and he got some kids from the retreat and he got a big birthday cake and they spread the word around. And Tony told me that around two o'clock the next morning the three bums came in and lo and behold the diner was filled with people! And they sang "Happy Birthday" to Rob. And Rob was so overcome when they presented him with the birthday cake that he was speechless for the moment. Then he collected himself and asked if he could take the cake home instead of eating it there; he wanted to take it home so he could look at it; no one had ever given him a cake before in his life.

After the party was over, there was an interesting conversation. The waiter leaned on his elbow on the diner counter and looked across at Tony and said to him, "I bet you belong to some church." And Tony, like the father in our parable, responded, "I belong to the church that throws parties for bums at two o'clock in the morning." The waiter looked at him and said, "If I could find such a church, I'd join it in the morning."

5

+

Zacchaeus

Luke 19:1–10

An elderly man was walking along the beach and he discovered and picked up a magic lamp. And of course, as everybody knows, when you find a magic lamp you rub it, and out came the genie. And the genie said, according to script, "Because you have released me from these thousand years of imprisonment in the lamp, you have whatever wish that you desire."

The man thought for a moment, and then he replied, "My brother and I had a fight some thirty years ago, and he hasn't spoken to me since. I wish he'd finally forgive me."

And there was a sudden thunder clap, a big puff of smoke, and the genie declared, "Your wish has been granted." And then he said, "You know, I've been around a long time. Most men would have wanted wealth and palaces and jewels." He went on, "I'm quite touched. You only wanted the love of your brother. Is it because you are old and dying?"

"No way," the man said, "but he is, and he's worth about sixty million."

It's like Leo Rosten's Jewish joke about what happened two days after Mrs. Nussbaum's funeral. The rabbi dropped in to

console the widower, and to his astonishment he found the bereaved on the sofa kissing a dazzling redhead.

"Nussbaum," said the rabbi, "your beloved is not even cold
in the grave and already...?"

He says, "In my grief, should I know what I'm doing?"

Of course, the source of the humor of the stories is the turn-
around. They give us an unexpected twist, and that's why we
laugh at them. But there's something similar in today's gospel.
There is a standard understanding which is quite valid. And
that understanding is that we have Zacchaeus, who is a dreadful sinner, one who is gouging the people and has become
wealthy by squeezing money out of them. He is a sinner. He is
a small man, both physically and morally. And he climbs up
the sycamore tree, and Jesus sees him; Jesus calls him down;
he converts, repents of his sins, and that's the end of his story.

And as I said, that's a perfectly good interpretation, but if
you listen to the story carefully there's another turn-around,
another reading that's quite possible here. One of the clues of a
different reading is what Zacchaeus has to say. He says, "*If* I
have defrauded any man..." He doesn't say he has. Notice he
has no admission of guilt in the story. He doesn't strike his
breast like another man in another story and say, "Oh God, be
merciful to me, a sinner." He simply says if he's done anything
wrong—with the implication that he really hasn't—he'll make
up for it. He does not beg for mercy, and he does not express
sorrow. Furthermore, Jesus makes no reference to repentance
and to conversion. And so there's a clue that maybe something
else is going on here.

Maybe it's possible that Zacchaeus, in fact, is a good man,
and his reputation for being evil is simply that: pure rumor
and backbiting, and lies. And in this interpretation, therefore,
what Jesus offers Zacchaeus is not forgiveness, but rather vindication. In fact in this reading Jesus says, "You are really not
what they say you are. You're all right in my book. I'll dine
with you."

In other words, what we have here is a Zacchaeus story that
can be read as being about a man who has been misjudged by

people, and to that degree he stands in a long, long history of those who would be misjudged.

In 1842, Congress didn't take Samuel Morse seriously when he explained to them his plans for a national telegraph system. In fact, Senator Smith of Indiana thought he might be mentally ill. In 1876, the president of Western Union laughed at Alexander Graham Bell, calling his telephone a useless toy. In 1878, the British Parliament ridiculed Thomas Edison's plans for an electric light, calling his invention unworthy of the attention of the scientific community. In 1908, people scoffed at Billy Durant for suggesting that someday it might be possible that cars would replace the horse and buggy. In 1940, military experts scoffed at the notion that the helicopter could possibly be of any kind of military use.

And so it is, you see, with this whole system here in the gospel text. What you have is people who've got an impression about Zacchaeus that is way off the mark, and Jesus sees through the rumors and the reputation to this man of a good heart. And it's only people who have a deep and abiding religious sense who have the ability to do that. And so the story turns around and says, if you think about it, that if anybody needed forgiveness, it was those who accompanied Jesus and who had prejudged poor Zacchaeus, those saying that he was a sinner when, in fact, he was innocent. And so Jesus offered Zacchaeus vindication and acceptance where others had judged him wrongly.

This interpretation opens the story in such a way that we can all put ourselves in at least two vantage points in the narrative—we can be with Zacchaeus, "up a tree," as we say popularly, or we can be on the ground with those who judge Zacchaeus wrongly. We've all been up that tree. The times you were misjudged. When people said you said things that you never said. When nasty rumors were attached to your name, and no matter how much you explained or what you did, people still believed them even though you were innocent.

Members of your own family who backbite you. Brothers and sisters who haven't talked to each other for years because of a misunderstanding. Finding yourself sometimes unfairly excluded from certain groups because of what they believe about you, which is not true. Frustrated, that for all the explanations that you give, people will refuse to believe otherwise. In that sense, the story of Zacchaeus resonates with us because maybe most of us at one time or another have been "up a tree."

On the other hand, most of us at one time or another have been on the ground. We have been the accusers, the rash judgers, those who have spread the gossip; we were glad to spread the evil word and were delighted at someone else's misfortune; we made innuendoes and feigned horror at the situation, but all the while we caused people to think less, or evil, of someone else. Simply put, we wronged someone. We misjudged them. And perhaps very, very badly at times. Some people may carry that on their consciences.

In either case, the gospel message is there. First of all, it offers the vindication by Jesus for those who have been wrongly judged. To everyone who has been slandered and rumored against and spoken evil of, it says that people look at appearances but God reads the heart. What this gospel offers is vindication. If no one else will break bread with you, Jesus says, "Come down, I'll dine at your house tonight." If no one else will believe you, Jesus says, "I've looked through the appearances and I see a good heart." If no one else will understand that you've turned around and given up your sins, Jesus does. If no one else takes you at your word, he does.

So for all the times you've been like Zacchaeus, up in a tree, and you have been wounded by other people's misinterpretation of your words and deeds, what the gospel offers is the one who really counts, the bottom-line person in your life who looks into your heart and loves you deeply; and vindicates you; and will announce that to the court of heaven someday.

And second, of course, if you and I are on the ground making the rash judgments and spreading rumors, and not defending our family and friends, this gospel offers forgiveness.

So when you read it this way, what the gospel comes down

to is invitation. It asks you to accept the Lord Jesus. To accept his vindication or to accept his forgiveness. In either case, the bottom line of the gospel is "mercy is at work."

And that's why we call the gospel the good news.

6

＋

Naaman: A Different Way

2 Kings 5:1–26

Let's begin by reviewing the situation depicted in this scripture. Naaman is a general in the Syrian army, and the Syrians are occupying Palestine. Naaman, as a general, is famous, well-respected, rich, a man of position, but he has one fatal flaw: he has leprosy, that dreaded, deadly disease.

He has been told by one of the captive Hebrew girls that there is a prophet named Elishah in Palestine who will cure him. So Naaman gets his retinue together, and he gets a lot of gifts, and he appears at the prophet's door, expecting the prophet to come out and cure him.

And immediately two things discourage Naaman. First of all, the prophet doesn't come out. He sends a messenger. And Naaman is very insulted. "I mean, after all, I'm a man of position. Why couldn't the prophet himself come and lay his hands on me and cure me?" And the second thing that disturbs him is the content of the message. And the content of the message is: "Go and wash seven times in the Jordan."

Now Naaman is from Syria, and in Syria they have two very lovely, sparkling rivers beside which the Jordan is a mudhole.

And so Naaman says, "Don't I have these lovely rivers in Syria? Why should I go in some little, dinky mudhole and dip myself seven times?" And he turns on his heel to go home.

But he's prevailed upon, literally and figuratively, to get down from his high horse and do what the prophet said, as long as he's come this far. And that's where our story picks up. He goes into the Jordan, dips seven times, and is cleansed, and now he adopts the God of Palestine, the God of the Hebrews—Yahweh.

So what does the story say to us? Can we translate it to our lives? I think we can because, fundamentally, the story is about invitation. Invitation to try another way, to get off the high horse that we think is so important, and the control that we think is so necessary, and let God enter in ways that we least expect.

Let me share with you the stories of three people who found a different way.

In the last century there were two very famous infidels, agnostics, who made a profession of mocking Christianity. They were on a train one day, and one of them said to the other, "People are still enamored of Christianity and this man Jesus Christ. You're a writer. Why don't you write a book exposing Jesus for the fraud that he is?"

The man who made the suggestion was Colonel Robert Ingersoll. Again, a very famous agnostic who used to go around giving lectures against Christianity. His companion, also an agnostic, was General Lew Wallace.

So Wallace, being a thorough man, began to research his book to expose Christ. To do that he had first to read the Bible. Second, he did some background reading. Finally, he went to the Holy Land, and for the first time in his life, he ceased to speak only to the university sophisticates of his time, the literati, and began to talk to the little people who have great faith. And at the end of his exploration, as you well know, he wrote his book *Ben Hur*. In that book, one of the sayings that is very important is one that arose at the end of Jesus' life when the centurion said, "Truly, this is the Son of God."

And General Lew Wallace did something he never thought

he could do. He got off his high horse and was able to declare Christ as God's Son, and became a believer.

The second story is a homely one. In these days when we're listening to the baseball games, I thought of Harmon Kille-brew, who finally made the Hall of Fame in 1984. I was struck with his little speech and I clipped it out. In his acceptance speech, when he was asked why he was such a great ballplay-er, he mentioned that his father used to spend hours and hours playing with him and his brothers outside on their little farm in Idaho.

He said, "I remember one incident." He said one day his mother came out to protest that all of his base running and all of his chasing grounders was ruining the grass.

And he said, "I'll never forget my father's reply. He turned to my mother and he said, 'Mary, we're not raising grass here. We're raising boys.'"

And he said, "Just that insight, just that homely little insight made me think that when I grew up I would not just have a house that nobody could touch; and furniture that nobody could sit on; and clothes that had to be perfect; and things that would be great artifacts for 'my castle.' But I would have a home for my children, and things would never get in the way of people."

Just that little incident helped him to see life in a different way.

And the final story I thought of when I was reading this sto-ry of Naaman is one about a woman named Mary Brenner. Ten years ago Mary Brenner was a forty-eight-year-old di-vorced mother of seven children. She worked in Beverly Hills. She had some kind of a carbon paper manufacturing company. She dealt with all the movie stars. She went to their parties. She hobnobbed with the celebrities, the kind of people whose faces leer at us out of *People* magazine.

What turned her around and made her see life differently? She came across a very famous photograph you and I have seen many times. The photograph was taken during the Holo-caust and is of the people lined up; a little eight- or nine-year-old boy is standing with his hands up and a Nazi is pointing a rifle at the kid, whose little eyes show deep fear and bewilderment.

And she looked at that photograph and suddenly realized that life could never be the same for her. She felt an enormous compassion for all those who were victims of other people's brutality, for those who were the most marginal.

So she went to the bishop of San Diego and said, "I'd like to have some kind of a little religious order here, and I'd like to dedicate myself to those people nobody wants. Who are the most deprived?"

And she wound up being called Sister Antonia, and she works with the women in the Tijuana Prison, a women's prison in Mexico, certainly the most abject and forlorn and neglected segment in humanity. She's their friend, companion, sister, mother, grandmother, all wrapped in one.

But again, notice her reaction. She has a story that literally goes from riches to rags because she saw something different. And when you reflect on the story of Naaman, that's its message, I believe. That Naaman, this great and noble and mighty general, had to let go and get down from his high horse, and try a way that fundamentally was humiliating for him. And he protested that. It was like struggling with the first step of AA. He protested that there was a power greater than himself. He knew he couldn't control his leprosy. He, the general, just had to surrender—surrender to something that he never thought he'd surrender to: the power of God in the message of the lowly prophet.

And so General Lew Wallace surrendered, and Harmon Killebrew surrendered, and Mary Brenner surrendered. And all this says to you and me that Jesus is always inviting us to another way. We think we have to be in such control. If things bother us, there is always psychiatry and medicine. Fine, they're great helps, but they're not the whole picture, as we well know.

And sometimes, fundamentally, like the lepers in the gospel story, we just have to let our pride go, and go to the Master and say, "Lord, have pity on me."

Each one of us has a spot of leprosy—some immoral spot somewhere, some defect somewhere—and we need healing terribly. And we can try all the sophisticated ways in the world, and we should, I suppose. But the scripture is inviting us, saying, "Can you be humble?"

It's inviting us to the way of the mystics and the prophets and the saints. It says, "Can you get down on your knees?"

Maybe the story of General Lew Wallace says, "Can you spend ten minutes a day reading scripture?"

And like General Wallace, will you find the person you've always been seeking? Can you give Christ that much time?

Perhaps, like Mary Brenner, you have to spend time—ten or fifteen minutes a day in meditation—looking at the horrors of the world, but saying, "I can do something. I can touch someone. I can make a difference."

Or maybe like the lepers in the gospel story, you and I gotta get down on our knees and go to confession and say, "Here I am. God, be merciful to me, a sinner. You see, Jesus, I have this spot of leprosy. I have this broken relationship. I have this nasty temper. I have this lustful impulse. I have this particular addiction. I have said things that should not have been said, and I have done things that I'm not proud of." So we have to get down and look at our situation in another way—maybe from the bottom up.

Maybe that's the story. The lepers had to see it from the ground up. And the word "ground" in Latin is *humus*, and that's the basis of the word "humility." And Naaman, as long as he was up there, couldn't see things in a different way, and he had to get down into the mudhole, seven times, yet. When he did that, things opened up. And his particular leprosy, whatever it might be, was cleansed.

So it's a time of renewal. Time for you and for me to say to the Lord Jesus, "Here I am."

That's the nice thing about being Christians standing before the Lord. Every one of us is equal. Your status, your income, your job, and your talents don't matter. You and I are equal before the Lord, saying, "Lord Jesus, have pity on me. I've got this thing that needs to be handled. As important as I am in this community, or this world, I'm going to get down on my knees, and from a different point of view, I'm going to cry out."

So listen to the story of Naaman, the general on horseback. Don't disdain what you think is beneath you. Don't disdain prayer or confession or reading scripture. Don't dismiss any prophet, however humble, who comes with the hidden word of God inviting you to see life from another angle, from the position of powerlessness, from the insightful posture of humility.

7

✛

John: The Disquieting Prophet

Matthew 3:1–12

This is a stern gospel surely. But more than that, it is a disquieting one because the prophet is brushing too close to us, threatening the soft defense of us good people. To see what I mean, we first have to take a look at the bad people: the deranged, the wicked, the unbalanced people, the doers of horrendous deeds.

You read about the man who the day before yesterday burst into the home of his ex-wife and shot her and her new husband and his own two daughters and then turned the gun on himself. Or not long ago, we heard about the young man in Montreal who burst into a classroom and shot and killed eleven women before destroying his own life. Or we've been reading about people who have been abusing little children to the point of torture and death.

Then there's the recent revelation in the communist bloc countries as a result of the dramatic break for freedom. The communist ideal is that everyone is equal. The communists even disdain titles and call each other by the equalizing term "comrade" so there will be no distinctions. Yet one of the reasons why communism has collapsed is the simple one that such governments cannot feed the people. So now it comes out that while the masses were literally starving and living in grinding poverty, some of the leaders of the Soviet bloc countries were living high on great secret estates, stashing away millions of dollars with plenty of food in their hideaways.

And when we hear of these things, these dark terrors that boggle the mind, we are affected in two ways that relate to this gospel. First, we are stunned and numbed by the sheer horror of it all. It's hard for any of us to conceive of how you can pick up a rifle and shoot human beings, and serially at that. What kind of derangement, what kind of craziness must that be? It's hard for most of us to conceive of selling cocaine to grammar school children. It's hard for us to conceive of what it must be like to be a hired killer, to shoot someone in cold blood and then go to a restaurant and enjoy a fine dinner. These people we say are not immoral. They are amoral. They are spiritual zombies, spiritually dead. They are sick, pathological. As I said, we are numbed by that sort of thing. It's beyond our comprehension.

But the second way these horrors affect us is far more subtle, far more spiritually subtle if you will. The effect of such horrors is this: they tend to justify us. *They tend to sedate the call to deeper holiness.* By this I mean we say, "Well, for all the little peccadilloes that I do, for all the little mistakes I make, for all the tiny sins I commit, my God, I'm not anywhere *near* to picking up a rifle and killing little children!"

True enough, thank God. And to this extent, we come off fairly well. But that's precisely why this gospel disturbs. John the Baptist won't let us settle for such complacency. There's too much at stake when good people are content with the counterfeit comfort that they are good because they are not bad. So he vents his anger, notice, not on the crazies, but on the churchgoing people. We heard who was coming to him in this gospel: the scribes and the Pharisees and the Sadducees. Religious leaders, good people, faithful people. They obeyed the Law and they went to the Temple. Yet to these very ones John cries, "Hypocrites, how can you hope to escape the vengeance that is to come?" Let us be clear: John is castigating the sins of the good, not the horrors of the wicked. And that's disturbing to our complacency.

For example, we hear a great deal—and it's very easily spoken about in public these days—about alcoholism. But the drunkenness of Christians who are not alcoholic is hardly ever mentioned. In the old biblical translation Paul speaks about chambering and wantonness, or, as the new translation says, debauchery; we frown on that debauchery and then turn around and say nothing about peddling "safe sex" to our youth. Marital lapses are euphemisms for nasty infidelities. Motels near the airports service the married and harried executive. Smart business deals mask the dishonest transaction. The casual cheating and lying are there. Well, we say, these things are a part of life. But the fact is, they're a part of the lives of good people.

And so it is such good people who are the object of John's disquieting words. The deeds that disturb him are not the works of darkness, of people who never go to church. They are the self-destructive behavior of those who do. No wonder John was and is unpopular. His contemporaries eventually killed him. We ignore him. Or, rather, we cheer him on when he scolds the unkempt soldiers and conniving, quisling tax collectors and mumble soft rationalizations when he turns his gaze on us, the good people.

He challenges us. "Demonstrate to me," he says, "that you're repentant. Make friends with someone you're at odds with. Pick up the phone and talk to somebody you haven't talked to in months or years. Be the first to hold out the hand of reconciliation even though it gets slapped or rejected. Don't turn your head at shady dealings. Be willing to put some of your possessions on the line. Tithe, not out of your excess, but out of your substance. Add up your Christmas spending bills that you chalked up for presents and then slice off 10 percent and give it to the poor. Give evidence that you mean to re-pent." It's all there for us to hear, us religious people.

But note too: there's a soft and hopeful side to the message of this disquieting prophet. Behind his call to the repentance of the good stands the promise of pardon, stands the Pardoner. And not just a pardoner who is tight-lipped and annoyed like a debt collector or craven landlord snatching at last his long sought rent money, but a pardoner who is friend, a very Lamb of God, a persistent, warm, pursuing, and patient lover.

He's the kind of patient lover who comes to mind in the story that a prison chaplain friend of mine told me. He told me about a man whose son has been in jail for about six years. And he said that for the past three years, every single week the man's father has come and waited in line for the opportunity to visit his son. And every week for the past three years the son has refused to see his father. For whatever reason—hatred or shame or guilt or whatever. My friend didn't know why. But he said that the father nevertheless still comes every single week asking permission to see his son, waits in line every single week and the son still refuses to see him every single week.

This father is surely the reflection of the Lamb of God, the Hound of Heaven, the Christ who stands behind the prophet's disquieting and challenging words. We're coaxed and shouted at by John but only that we might fall into the hands of the one who does not grow weary of us and keeps asking for us even though we do not ask for him. We're challenged by John precisely because we are the good people from whom more should be expected, more must be demanded, and he will not allow us to hide behind those comparisons which water down our call to genuine and deep holiness of life.

Yes, we cannot fathom the wickedness of mass murderers, and we cannot fathom the sickness of spirit, mind, and heart of those who do the terrible things we hear about on television or read about in the papers. But we can fathom what's in our own lives and therefore know that we both deserve and need the words of Advent's disquieting prophet.

8

✝

Pride as Hypocrisy

Matthew 23:1–12

Two psychiatrists were at a convention boasting about their cases.

One asked the other, "What was the most difficult case that you solved?"

The other answered, "Once I had a patient who lived in a pure fantasy world. He believed that somewhere in South America he had a fabulously rich uncle who someday would leave him a fabulous fortune. Every day, all day long he waited for a letter with the good news from some fictitious attorney. He never went out or did anything. He just sat around and waited."

"Well," asked his friend, "what was the result?"

The psychiatrist stood tall and preened as he answered, "It was an eight-year struggle, but with determined skill and insight, I finally cured him."

"Amazing," rejoined his friend.

"Yes. And then that stupid letter arrived...."

That's an old Milton Berle story. Here's one that's more clerical.

When I was a seminarian going to school in Baltimore, one

of the churches had become temporarily vacant due to the death of the pastor. To fill the gap they were bringing in some outside preachers for the novena. There was this young fellow, just fresh out of the seminary—we all knew him—who was invited to be one of the guest speakers. And there was no doubt about it. He sincerely believed that he was the greatest thing to hit the circuit since Bishop Sheen. He was like that as a student.

Well, he was introduced at the service, and he strutted up from the back of the church, smiling, almost a tad arrogant. He went to the pulpit quite ready to dazzle the peasantry. But, as I can tell you, one of worst fears of the public speaker was realized. He had forgotten his well-prepared notes. And forgetting his notes, he stumbled and stammered through his sermon. He must have been glad when it was over, and he lost no time in retreating back down the aisle with a rather long face. As he was going by, a dear old Irish lady tugged him by the sleeve and stage-whispered, "Lad," she said, "if you had come in the way you went out, you would have come out the way you went in."

And we're delighted with such stories. We like to see bubbles burst and people get their comeuppance. Indeed, pride goes before a fall.

But pride is a many-faceted evil. In the gospel before us it is expressed as gross hypocrisy. Such hypocrisy usually shows itself in two ways. One way is the simple and direct reality that people do not practice what they preach. That's it. That's pure and simple hypocrisy. Jesus and many others before and after him have observed angrily that such people say one thing and do another—often to the harm of many. The second way hypocrisy shows itself is more evil. This is when people not only do not practice what they preach but don't even believe what they preach. They say things out loud they don't really believe, but for political or social reasons they say them anyway. To put it bluntly, this is the hypocrisy that lies.

Why do they do this? Well, hypocrisy, as we've indicated, is an aspect of pride. It is that terrible pride that makes us say things that lie beyond our deeds. It is pride that makes us say things for appearance's sake, things we don't personally believe in or practice. It is pride that makes us cover up our dark deeds with fine words. It is pride that wants the first place of honor without honor. It is pride that wants the accolade, the title, without the integrity. It is pride, in short, that is behind hypocrisy and fuels hypocrisy. And I guess the worst kind is religious hypocrisy, which is why Jesus was so hard on the Pharisees, the religious leaders of the day. It is worse because it is not expected from those who are officially religious; it is worse because it is so subtle.

The late Cardinal Spellman's biographer notes that the cardinal indeed did many good deeds, but one of his weaknesses was his pride. One of the reasons he would not support John F. Kennedy was his insistence that he, Cardinal Spellman, was *the* prominent Catholic in the United States, and he did not want anyone else around to compete with him. Or, in a different vein, there's Alan Paton's delightful story of the rabbi, the cantor, and the Jewish janitor. The Days of Atonement came and, as required, the rabbi stood in the synagogue and did the traditional gesture. He struck his breast and intoned three times, "I am nothing. I am nothing. I am nothing." Then the cantor took his turn. In a well-modulated voice he sang, "I am nothing. I am nothing. I am nothing." Then the poor, humble Jewish janitor, observing this, also struck his breast and said, "I am nothing. I am nothing. I am nothing." And the rabbi turned and said to the cantor, " Look who thinks he's nothing!"

There is another reality that some people call hypocrisy, but it really isn't and we ought to explore it because it's more common than we think. This refers not to people who don't practice what they preach or believe what they preach. It refers to a kind of in-between, gray area that is, at bottom, noble. It refers to the person who practices what he or she preaches but not out of total conviction or maybe with minimal conviction and comfort. This person keeps up appearances, says prayers, and goes to Mass routinely, not to deceive but to search and ultimately to hope.

Let me explain. This is the person, let's say, who has some genuine difficulty about faith or practice. These are intellectual problems or problems relating to feelings. This person says: "How can I believe in a God who allows babies to be born with AIDS? How can I prove God's existence? How can God mean anything to me, or going to Mass mean anything to me since I lost my dad or my child? Since my spouse left me? Since my prayers for so many, many years have gone unanswered? I pray, such as it is, but it's like I'm talking to myself. I go through the motions; I go to church; I receive communion with my kids, but I'm not sure anymore. I'm just not sure. So much has changed. So much has happened. What am I doing here? I don't think I really believe. I'm empty, dried up. Everyone else seems to be born again, believing in visions and appearances. They turn their lives over to God and smile. I never have those experiences. I've never had a vision in all my life or heard a voice. Where was God when I needed God most? What am I doing here going through the motions? I feel like a hypocrite!"

But this is different. This is not the pride of hypocrisy. This is journey and search, which have an honorable place in the Christian tradition. This is the discipline of someone keeping up appearances, not to deceive, but to test; not to win applause, but to win some kind of sign from God that God is there and really cares. This is the journey of the spiritually numb hoping for a thaw. This is the dull routine of fidelity to religious practice even when the practice says nothing at the moment. This is the quiet, joyless duty of people going through the traditional "dark night of the soul." They're trying to be faithful even when they don't get anything out of it. Such people are not hypocrites. They are searchers after truth. They are beautiful. They are beloved of God, who is with them on their personal Calvary.

Do such people have a patron saint? Yes, and surely it must be old Simeon of the gospels, the man who for thirty years came to the Temple every day looking for the Messiah and who for thirty years went away disappointed. Who came out of duty, out of hope, out of need, out of simple routine. Who eventually got bored, who got nothing out of being faithful to the Temple and the Law; but, unknown to himself, all the while he was giving much. His was true worship with the focus away from his joyless self and totally on the search for God's Chosen One. That's why eventually he got to look into the face of the Messiah, cradle him in his arms, and sing his great song of thanksgiving. For him one day it all came together. As it will for all people like him.

These people are not hypocrites. They are not full of pride. If anything, they are full of humility. They are, in a word, faithful. Not for them will Christ shout out "Hypocrites!" because they say one thing and feel another. No, for them his words will be, "Enter thou into the joy of the Lord, my good and faithful servants."

9

✛

Capital Sins

Luke 19:45–48

As I pondered this gospel text about the money-changers being cast from the Temple, I began to reflect upon what we once called the capital sins, a term we sometimes still use. In the incident of the cleansing of the Temple two of those capital sins are most prevalent, and both are especially important to ponder at Lent.

For those of you who are old enough to remember, there are seven capital sins. The reason they're called "capital" is because the word "capital" means a source or a font, and if you get into these sins they so easily spill over and are a source or a font for dozens of others. You open this door and a lot of other things come in.

The two of these seven capital sins that came to mind were avarice and sloth. Let's begin by reflecting on avarice.

Fundamentally, avarice is centered around two poles. One is getting and the other is spending. If you want popular figures to relate to, you might turn to Dickens and think in terms of Ebenezer Scrooge, who, obviously, is one who keeps on getting and hoarding, and Dickens's Micawber, who is a kind of spendthrift.

It is interesting to realize that if you put the gospel on a computer, you'll find that the sin that Jesus mentions most in the four gospels is avarice—the danger of riches and greed. Far beyond anything else that he says, this persistent theme comes back and back. And I think he does that because all of us recognize that there's something about avarice that does much more than anything else to make us brittle and hard people.

Sometimes we speak of the vices as being cold or warm. People can relate to the warm vices, such as drinking or evil thoughts and things of that nature, but this is a cold vice. It makes people less human and causes them to drop out of the human community. Writers have long given us paradigms of such people, people like Citizen Kane who goes to the top and in the process hurts every human being along the way.

It is not without reason that all of the studies have shown that in past years the most successful men in business, the ones who were driven, who achieved extraordinary success, also have had an extraordinarily high divorce rate and have tended not to relate well to their children. Well, they were giving so much energy climbing to success that they didn't have time to form human relationships. So avarice becomes a very serious sin, and the source of so many others.

It might be worthwhile to reflect that fear is at the root of Scrooge's hoarding, his inability to share with the human community, and it is at the root of Micawber's spending and saying he's above it all. For Scrooge, and all like Scrooge, it is the fear of a childhood that was deprived, and the determination "that what I didn't have as a child, I'm going to grab and hold onto now as an adult," and so his kind of people turn in on themselves, and unless they're lucky enough to meet a Jacob Marley, they become subhuman, as did Scrooge.

Micawber's fear is of vulnerability. "If I have so much money and so much material wealth, and I can consume so much, if I can show the rest of the world that I'm above it all, then let other people, let the peasants worry about taxes and unemployment; but I can just consume and spend because I don't have to be vulnerable. I don't need anybody. I'm a self-made man, a self-made woman. I'm above it all. I'm above everybody." And, of course, this person becomes a machine.

Christianity, if anything, is a religion of vulnerability, and the person who is a spendthrift, the person who throws away money and consumes conspicuously, as we say, is afraid of intimacy and afraid of being vulnerable.

The antidote for avarice, of course, is poverty. Poverty is a complex thing, and here I'm not using the word to refer to being destitute, for poverty in that sense is no virtue. Rather, here I'm using the word to refer to letting go of things for the sake of the Kingdom. And that's where we start examining ourselves in Lent about avarice, you and I. What have we made our idol? What have we clung to at the expense of kindness, decency, and humanity? Let me share with you two examples.

One was told to me by my sister, a teacher. She had this little eight- or nine-year-old boy who was showing signs of illness and so she finally said, "Hey, this kid looks sick."

She sent him to the nurse. The nurse said, "Yeah, you've got flu, you've got a temperature. I'm going to have to call your Mom. Go home and rest, and she'll take care of you."

So she called the mother and the mother said, "Look, I've got my day planned out. That's your problem," and she hung up.

There's avarice. She couldn't let go of her time or her day, or whatever she had planned, for the sake of the Kingdom, which in this case happened to be a little child. See what avarice means to us?

The other example is about a woman I know. All her life long she had wanted a mink stole, and finally after many years of cajoling she got the mink stole just in time to go to an inaugural ball for a certain organization. She got herself dressed up in a beautiful evening gown. She proudly put on her mink stole. Her husband was in his tux. They were ready, just as in a fairyland story, to go to the ball as the prince and princess. And just as they were about to step out the door, one of their little kids gets sick, throws up all over the floor and is just deadly ill. Without blinking an eye, the woman takes off her mink stole, throws it over the banister, and stays home and takes care of the child. And even though they're fairly wealthy people she has the virtue of poverty, because poverty asks, "What can you let go of for the sake of the Kingdom?"

So the questions avarice asks are: What are you and I holding on to that we so badly need for our identity? What makes us less kind and forgiving and human? What is the idol that we have set up for ourselves that we keep worshiping at the expense of saying "I love you" and "I'm sorry" and holding hands and putting our arms around our children? Why are we so interested in success and making so much money that we cannot pause to look into the eyes of our spouse?

So you see, avarice just isn't one of those foreign or medieval sins that makes us think of those very extraordinary people like Scrooge or Micawber. If you look around the world, avarice is much intact.

The other sin I thought of is sloth. It's an interesting sin. The reason that it's interesting is that we often misunderstand sloth. When people talk about sloth as a capital sin, right away they think of laziness. And I would tell you, from observing all of us, the one thing we're not is lazy. As a matter of fact, one thing we probably should pray for during Lent is to learn how to be lazy because we run and move and we're so active and we just don't pause to smell the flowers.

But sloth is a kind of living death. Let me explain. As a lad, Bruno Bettelheim, the psychoanalyst, lived in Germany, and at that time the Nazi terror was starting to move through Germany, and the signs were clear that it was going to engulf Bettelheim and his Jewish family.

He wrote a book called *The Informed Heart*. He tells in that book how he and his peers pleaded with the elder people to flee Germany, run away, because this terror was at their door. But the more they pleaded the more the old people said, "No, we can't leave our possessions, we can't leave our homes, we're settled here."

And this went on week after week until finally the young

people left and the Nazi terror came and swallowed up those Jews and killed them. That is an example of sloth, and it yields a good definition of sloth that applies to many of us.

Sloth is when one knows that one is set upon a damaging or deadly course and somehow cannot muster the courage, the hope, and the faith to do something different. The man who detests his job but continues in it for a lifetime is guilty of sloth. The woman who sees herself as a martyr to her family, the grownup child who never makes a break with his or her parents, the married couple whose marriage is a life-long hell, the teenager whose crowd is leading him or her to drugs or drink or premarital sex—they're all guilty of sloth. They know they're on a damaging course. They know they're going to just die from this. They know it's utterly destructive for themselves and everybody else, but they can't bring themselves to get out of it. As a matter of fact, the one thing that the slothful have in common is the perfect alibi.

If you should mention, as I have done to some of these people, that they might possibly have a different reaction and way of life, they come upon you with a ton of excuses and anger. The man who is in this terrible job he hates, and it's giving him ulcers and is going to shorten his life by twenty years, will say, "But I've gotta support my family."

The martyred housewife will say, "But how can my kids do without me if I'm not there every moment? How will they make the bed? How will they find the refrigerator? How will they work the microwave oven? How will they have clean clothes?"

And you say, "Well, at some point they've gotta be on their own. How old is your little boy?"

"Well, twenty-eight."

But you see what's happening here? The grownup child says, "Well, I can't leave because my parents need me."

Teenagers know that they are going to destroy themselves with the drugs or the drink, but the need for popularity and acceptance is so great that they don't have the courage to move away. And that is sloth.

How do we know that we're guilty of sloth? We know that we are guilty of sloth when we find ourselves continually depressed or in pain, and can produce excellent moral and practical reasons why we can't improve our lot. Now, if any of you are guilty of that, it's a serious fault.

It doesn't help, of course, if you're a distorted Christian, because if you're a distorted Christian you probably have learned that suffering is what we're here for. What are we here for? We're here to suffer. Some God. So therefore I will put up with this because I will be holy and I will be a good Christian because nothing more is asked of us in this valley of tears, in the abyss of misery, than to suffer.

Somebody got a message across that Christians are supposed to be terribly unhappy and that unless you are suffering, you are a suspect Christian. We get it translated, of course, in common parlance when we say, as you and I do, "Mmm...boy, this really tastes good. It must be sinful. This is really neat. It must be sinful."

You see what you're relaying, the kind of theology you're working on? You're saying that you have a masochistic God who wants nothing more than for you to writhe in pain; you're saying your pain is a sign that you're doing God's will. This is hardly the God who gives us beautiful days, the God who hugs little children, the God who talks about flowers and birds of the air and the lilies of the field.

So there we are, reflections on two kinds of sin. Jesus casts out those in the Temple because they were avaricious. It's not so much that they were selling things; it was that they had become so much like what they were selling. And others were guilty of sloth because they knew that was a destructive, immoral, and irreligious thing, having so much commerce in the center of the Temple; but nobody had the courage to stop it.

So in the middle of Lent we ask: "Are we avaricious?" To find out you only need ask yourself: Do I give more importance to things than to people? In the past year have I given so much energy to some project and to success that I have not measurably grown in human kindness and relationship?

And to find out if we are slothful we need only ask: What destructive or deadly course am I on that I have the perfect alibi for? When am I going to make a move to do something different and change? The point is that we really can change.

And a good place to start that change is prayer. Avarice and sloth, old-fashioned terms, are ever-present realities to pray over. Through prayer we can examine ourselves and turn to the Lord of love and beauty and joy, and say, "I've got to change. Speak, Lord, and tell me how."

10

+

Weeds and Wheat

Matthew 13:24–30

Catching a bit of old newsreel the other night on television, which was background to the current Arab uprising, I realized how familiar and, unfortunately, how casual the scene had become to all of us. In the newsreel there were the distressingly usual pictures of armed soldiers on the plains and heights of Mount Sinai as Israel, Jordan, and Egypt were at it again in war. But because that scene was so familiar I wondered if people were looking beyond the political event and realizing that they were looking at a spiritual event, or rather at one of the centers of that event. Anyway, there was something in the newsreel, as the camera swept Mount Sinai, that caught my eye. It was just a passing camera shot but one that forcibly reminded me of today's gospel parable. First, a little background.

Mount Sinai is on a desert triangle about 150 miles wide. This triangle is wedged in between Asia and Africa. Its northern edge touches the Mediterranean Sea. On the west is the Gulf of Suez and the Suez Canal, and on the east is the Gulf of Aqaba. But within, most of the peninsula is a desert that turns into rocky plateaus and in turn gives way to a granite mountain chain on the south.

Here, among these granite peaks, is the "Jebel Musa," or the Mountain of Moses, the 7000-foot peak that is traditionally associated with the place where Moses spoke to God and received the Ten Commandments. Scholars have no way of knowing the exact location of this site, but old Jewish and Christian tradition have placed it here at the point called the Mountain of Moses. And here, too, at its base, is where God appeared to Moses in the burning bush. Here the God of Abraham and Isaac and Jacob was revealed. Here God gave Moses his commission to lead the people to freedom. It was on these plains that water came from the rock and manna fell from the heavens. It was at this mountain, when the Hebrew slaves fled from Egypt, that they made a covenant with God. It was from this mountain that they were welded into a nation and left as soldiers to invade Palestine.

Well, the soldiers are still there today. Only today the soldiers are Israelis. In the past they have been Egyptian, British, French, Arabian, Saracen, Ottoman, and what have you.

But also today something else endures, that which in the newsreel caught my eye, that which stands at the foot of Mount Sinai. For looking more like a fortress than anything else is St. Catherine's monastery. Here a handful of Greek Orthodox monks keep vigil at the mountain in a life of prayer, work, and assistance to pilgrims.

The Roman emperor Justinian built this monastery in the sixth century, but it had been a place of pilgrimage many, many centuries before that. In 342, St. Helena, the mother of Constantine, visited the site; and many holy hermits had been living in many caves there for a long time.

Since at one time the Muslim nomads had been a threat to the monastery, the monks built the great walls surrounding it. Now these same Bedouin nomads help the monks at their work and care for pilgrims. In the library of the monastery are priceless manuscripts. One of the more dramatic stories was the finding of a genuine fourth-century scroll of the New Testament and most of the Old Testament. It was found all heaped up in a garbage can. Today the scroll is in the British

Museum. The whole fantastic discovery was, at least among scholars, like finding the Hope Diamond in a glass factory.

Behind the monastery is a flight of four thousand steps leading to the top of the mountain. These four thousand steps were built by a long-dead monk as a penitential project. There is also a mummified figure of a hermit named Stephen near the steps. He is a silent testimony of the vigil that the monks of St. Catherine's have kept for fourteen centuries over the holy mount of Sinai.

And all of that, monastery and mortar, is behind those casual pictures of Mount Sinai which formed the background for a terrible and drawn-out war. But more than that, the whole scene is in fact a living parable of today's parable. Mount Sinai is surely a living monument that weeds and wheat, military and monk, have coexisted for an awfully long time. That alongside the glories of God's revelation to Moses are the shames of wars, deceit, and mistrust. Depending on your point of view, you'll be a cynic or a believer.

The cynic will bypass Moses and the manna and the Exodus and God's deliverance and God's word and the paschal lamb and the Law and will remark that, well, after all these centuries, what are the results? After all these centuries, what do we have on God's so-called holy mountain? Armed soldiers and death-dealing tanks.

The believer responds, yes, but notice, we have a monastery there too; we have monks; we have prayer; we have care. The believer, with one eye on today's gospel, remarks that God is apparently forbearing and enormously tolerant, for God is letting us share the same mountain:

Moses and generals
manna and K rations
law and license
liberation and slavery
monks and soldiers
weeds and wheat, if you will.

The believer will say that someday all will be well on Mount Sinai. Someday Moses will recruit the generals; monks and soldiers will break bread together rather than K rations; all slavery will turn to liberation; and St. Catherine's rather than armed camps will survive. Yes, the persistence of that monastery in the midst of the military is a sign—and the wisdom of the gospel.

For our part we must remember that we are the descendants of Moses; we are brothers and sisters to the monks at St. Catherine's—we are children of the ancient heritage. After all this time to this very day, we still listen to the word, break the bread, offer our prayers, and like the monks moving amidst the soldiers, keep alive that hope promised by the one who cautioned, "Let them grow together."

11

✠

Silence

Matthew 22:1–14

On the surface this is a gospel that evokes mixed feelings. I mean that perhaps like me you have always felt a twinge of resentment that the king should cast into the horrors of darkness a passer-by from the street because he was not wearing a wedding garment. After all, he *was* only a passer-by, someone suddenly accosted by the king's servants and pressed with an instant invitation to attend a sumptuous wedding feast—now.

He certainly did not go around carrying spare formal attire just to meet such an emergency. In fact, you might feel, in view of the original refusals, he was doing the king a favor by being there at all. And on top of this, the gospel makes it clear that the servants going into the streets indiscriminately gathered *all* the people they found, both the good and the bad; and, presumably, the well- and the ill-clothed. Why, then, should the king be astonished to find a man there minus a wedding gown? What did he expect?

Evidently the king did expect the man to have on his wedding garment and felt justified when he threw him into the awful darkness for not having it. Now if we suppose that the king was not Gilbert and Sullivan's Mikado or Captain Ahab or

Captain Bligh, was not demented or a fanatic about etiquette, then we must assume that some how, some way, the sudden guest really was at fault. Some commentators have suggested that wedding garments were provided at the cloakroom, and so guests would be at fault for refusing to wear theirs. Others have thought that the servants carried the garments with them and issued them to the prospective guests.

Whatever the case, our answer is certain: the man was wrong, not the king. We are certain of this answer because it is based on the most important sentence in this gospel, the sentence which gives us the key to the whole riddle, which puts the blame rightly where it belongs: squarely and unmistakably on the shoulders of the guest. And that brief, revealing sentence is: "But he was silent."

He was silent, notice. He had not one word to say in his own defense, as surely he would have if he were unjustly accused and if his silence would cast him outside into the terror. He had nothing to say: no excuse, no explanation, no protest. He's like Ralph Kramden on the "Honeymooners" when he blows the whole thing and struts behind Alice making gestures and moving his lips but no words come. He blew it. He knows it and she knows it. There's nothing he can say. So with our man in the gospel. He had nothing to say. Just a shrug of the shoulders, raised eyebrows, empty gestures. But no explanation, no protest. His silence branded him as guilty beyond the shadow of a doubt. "But he was silent."

This whole gospel, as we all know, is a parable. It is a disguised story of God's announcement of his Son's love and the community he founded with its treasures of charity and grace. In the gospel, the man who preferred his farm represents anyone too attached to material things to seriously heed God's invitation. The man who went to his merchandise represents those with an overeager desire for shallow fame and gain. No time for the deeper things of life. Those who put to death the king's servants represent those who by excessive greed, lust, selfishness, and addictions slay even the most insistent messenger of God's call to repentance and entrance into the Kingdom.

Finally, there are those who did come to the wedding feast, those who have entered the Kingdom: the good, the bad, and the indifferent. Now, at the end of time, Christ who has been harboring all separates them. Entering the banquet hall of his Kingdom he spots the still unrepentant sinner, the still luke-warm believer, and says with initial sadness, "Friend, why are you not wearing a wedding garment? Why are you still sinful, still refusing my love, still unrepentant, still cold toward me?"

If any comment can be made it will be those four accusing, lonely words: "But he was silent." For who of us will really have an excuse when Christ comes to judge us? We are sur-rounded by his providence, taught by his church, nourished by his flesh, nurtured by his word, washed in his blood, coaxed by his Spirit and sought, hunted, and pursued in a mil-lion ways by that terrible, jealous love of his. We are the prey of the prodigal father, the coin of the housekeeper, the lost lamb of the shepherd, the chicks of his gathering, the feet of his washing. What explanation will we be able to give for our ulti-mate failure of love? What excuse? What protest?

None. "But he was silent."

Thus, the warning of the gospel. Yes, we have struggles. Yes, there are situations in our lives that make it almost too late to reverse our position. Yes, there are "circumstances," as we say. Oh, but deep down, all taken together, they're not enough of an excuse to flee conversion or to refuse a change of heart. Christ is still anxious to have us at the banquet. He still sends tireless servants: friends, the church, the sacraments, prayer, help in many guises.

The gospel says that if we continue to refuse God's invita-tion we will have, can have, no words of excuse to offer. Help-less silence will be the only posture.

But if you heed the gospel's warning and invitation, then words will flow; there will be stories of struggle to be sure, perhaps even of suffering, but there will surely also be words of triumph to gladden the heart of God already gladdened by your return home.

12

✝

Christmas Music

Luke 2:8–20

There was a tap for attention. Everything was eternally still. Nothing moved. Nothing breathed. Everything was poised, ready. The Great Conductor looked around at the stillness, peered at the mute readiness, and then began the majestic sweep of the music, a symphony the Conductor alone had composed.

First, there was the soft sound of the trumpets, growing louder as light appeared and the darkness retreated like the ebb of a giant wave.

Next, the violins painted a huge sky vault of blue around the light—the vault we call sky. With a point of the baton the Conductor called for the trombones to coax the appearance of dry land.

The clarinets told of the particular lights in the sky vault: the sun, the moon, the stars. The flutes and piccolos pinpointed the slippery fishes and winging birds. The drums and bass fiddles prodded the large animals roaming over the planet earth.

Then there was an infinite musical pause. Finally, the Conductor, with immense genius, drew the orchestra into one gigantic chord, sweet beyond telling, majestic beyond describing, unearthly and full of force as something of the Conductor himself seemed to pass into the music. Something of the Conductor's own personality passed into this chord, which burst into a whole new instrument, which we call man.

Hereafter, all things played their notes and produced their melody with perfection: the light, the sky, the land, the sun, the moon, the stars. The winged things and the roaming beasts on earth—all were flawless in their performance. The harmony was magnificent.

But especially pleasing to the Conductor was the Great Instrument, man, which played a most pleasing music, not only because there was something of the Conductor in him, but also because he was the only one there who could play freely.

Everything else was programmed, wound up as it were, by the Conductor and so simply had to play the tune. Man alone was left to himself. He was not made to play. He was indeed *invited!*

The movements of the symphony of creation flowed with rapture from one to another. It was beautiful music, giving delight and pleasure to all.

Yet—in the midst of a cascading crescendo, as the music rose to a thrilling climax, something happened! As obvious and indisputable as the sun in the sky, heard by one and all, a false note was sounded! The music, indeed everything, stopped dead. The Conductor stared, unbelieving. That false note—whence had it come?

Certainly not from the land trombones, not from the blinking clarinets, not from the swimming flutes or flying piccolos, not from the heavy drum or the plodding bass fiddles. All of these instruments had been prepared by the Conductor to play what he designed they would play. They were prewound, automatic, helpless to play other than that which was foreordained.

With silent and infinite intenseness the Conductor understood that the false note originated from the only free instrument that was invited to play, the only one that had choice and freedom to play a false note if he so wished: the Great Instrument, man.

The Conductor looked. The Great Instrument felt that look and was intensely ashamed that in a moment of pride, of madness, he deliberately sounded a false note.

But, now, what would happen? The instruments sat hushed, looking at one another, not daring even the most fleeting quarter note. They were silent, all of them, wondering: What would the Composer-Conductor do? There seemed to them two possibilities.

One: he would go on pretending that there was no false note. But that wouldn't work. Everyone had heard. Everyone knew. The insult itself was simply too obvious, too big, to pass by unnoticed. No, that false note cried out for apology.

Or the Conductor could simply scrap the whole score, disband the orchestra, do away with the whole symphony. Destroy it.

But no one counted on the genius of the Conductor, or perhaps we should say, the unlooked for mercy and love of the Conductor. For, putting down the baton, the Conductor did a very strange thing.

Carefully he reached out into the infinity and plucked the false note that would be forever vibrating in the atmosphere of time and eternity. The Conductor held the note before the orchestra and said to them: "Ladies and gentlemen, I am deeply offended by this false note. Deeply offended? No, I should put it more strongly. My heart hurts. It hurts because the one instrument that was so much a part of myself was the one to produce this false note which I now hold in my hand.

"Now, what shall I do? Forget? You know that this is impossible. Shall I dismiss the symphony, destroy my masterpiece, angrily grind your instruments into nothingness? [At this the oboe emitted a low, plaintive sigh.] But, no, ladies and gentlemen, I shall do neither."

Then, after what seemed like an eternal pause, the Conductor continued: "What if I take this false note and build a whole *new* symphony around it? *What if I rewrite the music to fit this note?* Then it won't be a false note any more. It will be a part of the music. It will start a whole new melody. This, then, ladies and gentlemen, is what I shall do. I shall write a whole new piece of music around this note."

And this is what the Great Conductor did do—rewrote the score and produced a new masterpiece, a new symphony, and the beginning of that masterpiece is called Christmas.

The disastrous false note of our sins ruined the original grand design, but God has taken our falseness and made it the start of something new. Another theme is introduced: a new beginning enfleshed in the New Adam, the new human being, Christ. This Christ is our second chance. He gathers all of our falseness, our brokenness, and begins a new song of praise, a new creation. He is the living, concrete forbearance, mercy, and kindness of God. He strikes a new note of forgiveness, harmony, and reconciliation.

Yes, we can cry out: We are unworthy instruments! We are false notes! We are dissonant sounds! And yet at the same time we can celebrate, for this God of ours loves us and has re-created a whole new symphony out of our falseness. Instead of emptying out the whole orchestra, this God emptied the God-head and became a helpless baby in a crib, and when that baby grew up he provided a whole new musical pattern of forgiveness and love.

All that is left for us at Christmas is to cry out with David's 103rd Psalm: "O Glory be to the Lord forever.... While life lasts in me, I will sing in the Lord's honor!" Or, we can join Luke's angelic choir and chorus: "Glory to God in the highest and on earth, peace to those on whom his favor rests."

13

✛

Epiphany

Matthew 2:1–12

Over the Christmas holidays, a grandfather brought his visiting grandson to church. Apparently he hadn't been to church too much so he had a lot of questions. So he whispers to grandpa, "What does it mean when they bring the basket up?"

Grandpa says, "That means they're giving their donations as gifts to the Lord."

"What does it mean when the people bring in that bread and wine?"

And he says, "Well, the priest, Father Bausch, will take the gifts of the people and they'll become the body and blood of Christ."

He says, "What does it mean when Father Bausch, after the gospel, holds up the book and kisses it?"

And he says, "That means a great deal of reverence for the word of God."

And he says, "What does it mean when Father Bausch takes his watch off and puts it on the pulpit?"

"Absolutely nothing, son, absolutely nothing!"

We have many questions—some of great moment and some of little consequence at all—about the liturgy and key days on the church's calendar, and one of the important questions is: What does Epiphany mean? As most of you know, Epiphany means revelation. It means a showing, a direction for our search. And interestingly enough, the scriptures imply it's a search that everyone must make. Luke, in his gospel, has the poor searching, in the form of the shepherds. Matthew, in his gospel, has the learned and the rich searching, in the form of the Magi. So the message is that there is room for everybody in this search, from no degrees to Ph.D.s, from shepherds to executives.

And so to the Magi. They are three searchers who did not find the answer to life in their horoscopes, but took a long and difficult journey to another country in search of the Christ. Now, we're used to that story, but you have to appreciate the decision that they made; to help us appreciate that decision the gospel gives us two sets of wise men, for contrast.

The first set are the ones we call the Magi. They have those lovely medieval names of Gaspar, and Melchior, and Balthazar. But there was the second group of wise men, the ones that Herod called in—the scribes and the Pharisees. He says, "I've got a problem here."

And when you've got a problem you call in the experts. And so he gathered the wise men and said, "They talk of the birth of a Messiah; I want to know where he is to be born."

And so these wise men, of course, came up with the answer. They said, "In Bethlehem of Judea."

And that's all that we hear of them. Except when this story is told, we never hear of those wise men. Why? Well, like so many, and unlike the Magi, their hearts did not follow their heads. They gave lip service and head service. You know, like, "I gotta look into this God question—someday. I've gotta try to figure out life's meaning—someday. I've got to be kinder and more forgiving—someday. Life is fundamentally about relationships and not possessions, and I gotta remember that—someday."

So this first group of wise men stayed aloof from life, from risk. And there was a risk, because, after all, suppose that they had gone on the journey and *had* found the Messiah. What changes would they have had to make in their lives? And so they thought it was better to talk about all this than to do something about it.

And then we have the Magi who took a risk, and it was a risk. There was the risk of inquiry: Who knew what they might learn? The risk of journey: Who knew what they might meet? And the risk of search: Who knew what they might find? Or better still, whom might they find? That was the risk of the journey.

And that's why the gospel is very challenging. It's not just a pretty story that conjures up in our minds oriental kings floating over the desert sands on the way to Bethlehem. The gospel is really saying something to us, and that, basically, is a challenge. We are asked to choose between the two types of Magi, the two kinds of wise men—those who play it safe and those who take the risk. Those who sit around and talk about it, becoming holier, better, deeper, more profound lovers of God; and those who do something about it.

And so that's why there's a question that's hooked into this gospel of the wise men. And the question is: What about you and me? Where do we fit into this gospel story in this Epiphany feast?

Well, the first thing that is very valuable that we can say, I think, is that we're part of a community, a church, a caravan. There is great wisdom in that. And you should be reminded of the great wisdom that you're showing in being a part of that caravan because no one on this entire earth can successfully journey alone. We need each other's guidance, we need each other's balance, and we need each other's encouragement.

And second, the idea that we're on a common journey also helps us to realize that we're in different spaces on this journey. Some of us are way up in front; some of us are in the rear; some of us are willing; some of us are foot-dragging. Some of us journey with great certainty. They've found Jesus. They've looked into the face of the Messiah. Others journey with great doubt. They're still trying to struggle with fundamental questions of sickness and death and hurt and broken relationships, and all the things that say there can't be a God if God is the one who allows babies to be born with AIDS or cancer.

We have those who are veteran seekers and those who are just newcomers to this caravan. I don't think that's important—where we are in the caravan. I just think that it's important that we are journeying at all, which means that at least we've responded to the gospel; we're taking the risk. And I think that's the best part of the Feast of Epiphany. And that's the best part of this caravan—what we call community. Because those among us who are vigorous can support those of us who are tired and just plain discouraged. And I see that all the time.

And those of us who are so certain can encourage those of us who are struggling with doubts—about faith, about God, about life, and about love. And those of who are devout can be a sign to those of us who are tepid and lukewarm. And those of who are young and innocent can signal hope to those who have borne the long journey.

So to me, Epiphany *is* a feast of hope. You give me courage, as I hope I do you. You encourage my faith where I'm weak, and vice versa. We look around our caravan and we have children, and we have octogenarians, and we have teenagers, and we have students. We have doctors and lawyers and Indian chiefs. And we have people who never got out of eighth grade. We have people whose relationships are whole, and people whose relationships are fractured. We have people of great virtue and people of great vice. No matter, you're a part of the caravan. You're journeying. This is Epiphany time, revelation time.

And just by that fact, let me give you Epiphany's promise: Wherever we are in this caravan, we will, everyone of us, reach the goal of the journey; that is, we too will look into the face of the Messiah.

14

✟

Counterculture

John 15:1–8

As you listen to the words of Jesus, you always have to appreciate just how different he is, and what difference he is calling us to. "Others come in, "he says, "as thieves and marauders," but he comes as a good and concerned shepherd. Others come to kill. He comes to give life and give it abundantly.

If Jesus were speaking today, in the 1990s, he would probably pick up the terminology of the sociologists and talk in terms that we hear so often: of culture and counterculture. And maybe to translate what he means in more modern terms, let me share three current news items that best describe the three pillars of our culture.

The first of these items is that in Sheridan, Arkansas, they've had terrible trouble because one, two, three, now four teenagers have committed suicide. That small community, as you can imagine, is just devastated. The reporters, of course, flocked out there with cameras and microphones at the local high school, thrusting them into the faces of the kids, asking "What do you think of it all?"

But a news article I read is more sober and suggests that much more basic questions are also being asked. It asks, "Have these youths somehow gotten involved in the occult? Does it go back to drugs, as most tragedies in most communities seem to do anymore? Might teenage suicides be another one of those incomprehensible teenage fads?" Then referring to that small town of Sheridan, Arkansas, the article comments:

> Not many years ago this community was one of those close-knit, self-contained, All-American small towns, sheltered to an extent from the corrosive winds of modernity by the great pine forests that circumscribe it. But by its earnestness it made its way into the mainstream, and now it has been strip-developed, sub-divided, Wall-Marted, fast-fooded into a conventional, white, suburban, middle-class town with only faint, fading identity. It could be any place in the country.
>
> Its youngsters are heirs now to the same pressures and anxieties that bedevil those in similar communities in Pennsylvania or Illinois or Texas. They use drugs, probably in the same proportion. They drive around at all hours with their car radios loud enough to wither the roadside dogwood blossoms, and they demand the same MTV and pump-up sneakers. For years the traditional teenage pastime was hanging-out. Then the adults got together, voted a sales tax three years ago, raised one million dollars, and built a recreation center to make life easier for the generation coming. And it surely has made life easier, but now they're killing themselves.

We pause and think about the writer's message. He suggests that the kids, to their harm, have been placed on the first pillar of American culture: materialism. Materialism has become so powerful a source of our identity that kids in ghettos literally kill other kids for their Reeboks or latest "in" jacket. Why? Because materialism is what America offers as the symbol of success. Without it, why live? It's a hallmark of our culture. But not Jesus' counterculture. "What does it profit one to gain the whole world and lose one's soul?"

The second pillar of our culture is consumerism. This next article I have perfectly describes this pillar. First, the problem. The problem is that children see an average of one hundred commercials every day and between thirty and forty thousand commercials a year. How to squeeze more of them into their four to seven hours of daily television watching? The answer to this challenge is what is called "video-power." Video-power refers to the breakthrough of seamlessly mixing television programs and commercials for kids. They're now blended in so well that you can't tell where the program begins and the commercial ends and vice versa. Commercial hawkers even play in the programs. Ronald McDonald, for example, is in a full-length program of *Treasure Island.*

The movies, of course, have done this in recent years; that is, they have hawked products. This article notes: *"Back to the Future II,* starring Michael J. Fox, stuck viewers with a shopping cart full of brand names: Toyota, Miller, AT&T, USA Today, Texaco, Black and Decker, U.S. Sprint Overnight Service, Pizza Hut, and Pepsi came up several times. Pepsi was quite pleased about that." I might add that you should also know that Disney Studios will, for twenty thousand dollars, put your product in their next movie. For forty thousand dollars they'll turn the label to the camera, and for sixty thousand dollars they'll have the hero or heroine use the product.

We haven't even mentioned the taken-for-granted cultural phenomenon of treating people like things, things to be "consumed." In a recent column Mike Royko wrote: "Sometimes I flip through the cable channels, pausing a few seconds at the major ones. Flip—there's somebody being shot or blown up. Flip—there's a couple of people stripping and hopping in bed. Flip—there's a couple of people in bed being shot or blown up. Flip—what a relief. It's a standup comedian. But what's that he's saying? The old 'F' word? Not once, not twice. Goodness, doesn't he know any other words?" Thieves and marauders of the mind!

Consumerism is taught from the earliest years and becomes the fabric of all that we do. It's a pillar of our culture and is denied by Jesus, who told countercultural stories, such as the one about the rich man who consumed and consumed, built bigger and bigger barns—and died one night without having loved anyone.

The third pillar of our culture is individualism. And the third and final article I have concerns a beloved comic strip fondly remembered: "Archie." The article is about a television show that offers an updated version of the comic strip. In the show, Archie and his friends—Veronica, Reggie, and Jughead—return as adults to Riverdale. There have been some changes. Archie is no longer a fine, wholesome guy. He's been talked into the yuppie, consumerist mainstream by his fiancée. Veronica has had at least four or five marriages and is now hunting Archie, trying to get him into bed with her. In the script is this dialogue:

> "But I have a fiancée," says Archie, trying to back off Veronica.
> "Don't worry," Veronica says unmoved, "I've had thirteen."

Jughead is a divorced psychiatrist trying to raise his alienated son, and Reggie is a money-crazed owner of a health club. Times have changed! Archie and his friends are no longer a community. They are exemplars of the third pillar of our culture: individualism. "I do my thing: run through spouses, children, jobs, relationships. They're all temporary. I'm the one who counts. The world revolves around me. I'm the center." But Jesus offers the countercultural advice that before we offer our gift at the altar, go back first and repair a broken relationship and heal a fractured community.

Just as the gospel stands in stark contrast to all this, so do some people. There is, for example, a married couple, Kathy and Mitch Finley, who recognize the seductiveness and the danger of the three pillars of our culture: materialism, consumerism, and individualism. They're trying hard to raise their children to be Jesus' counterculture. They're trying to keep out the thieves who come to steal their innocence and the marauders who come in to kill their spirit. They admit it's hard, but nevertheless they have some suggestions that I will pass on to you.

First they comment: "A culture's not something we can simply step aside from, or take off and put on, like a hat. A culture's more like something we inhabit, as a fish swims in the sea. In the dominant culture of the United States, it's taken for granted, among other things, that money and material possessions are the ultimate form of security and are central to one's values as a person; that violent means are an acceptable way to solve one's problems; that individualism and being self-sufficient are preferable to communal relationships; that doing, being productive are more important than being; that shopping is the number one form of recreation." And they too realize that such a dominant culture clashes with basic Christian principles.

At this point, you might be thinking, "Well, we've heard all this before and this is the stuff that we pay you, as the preacher, to get up there and tell us. We feel good to be harangued once in a while. But now we can go home and live as usual." But that's just the point. Can we? Educated and slick marauders and thieves are stealing our lives away, making us strangers to each other in the pursuit of materialism, consumerism, and individualism. Suicide, abortion, divorce, and AIDS are not minor commentaries on our culture. So, let's listen to the four suggestions of the Finleys on how to be countercultural.

First, they say, parents themselves must get their act together. They have to examine what they want, the nature of their relationship, and the values they want their children to have. They really have to think this through—together.

Second, the Finleys say, we have to change our lifestyle. I always like the story of the well-to-do people who moved next door to the Amish community. The Amish are standing there looking on in astonishment as they unload the moving van and out comes the radio, out comes the television, out comes the VCR, out comes the Jacuzzi, out comes the computer. And out of neighborliness, an Amish man says, "Look, if you ever have trouble with those, I'll be glad to help you out." "Oh," the new neighbor says, "thank you. You really know how to fix these things?" "No," the Amish neighbor says, "but we'll teach you how to live without them."

Third, the Finley's recommend that you turn off the television. It does have an "off" button. If you want people using the "F" word in your living room, keep the television on. If you want your children to be inundated with commercials and free-wheeling sex, leave it on. But if you want Christ's values, turn off the television.

Finally, they suggest that you read. Read about the faith. Take a few minutes or half-hour daily to do some good spiritual reading. Daily, ongoing secular messages cannot feed the soul. There needs to be some countercultural message getting through.

I suppose when you come right down to it, their advice, in everyday language, is about forgiveness, about eating at least three or four meals at home together each week, holding hands and praying together, taking our faith to the marketplace, asking someone to church, sharing faith in groups.

So what do we have? We have the culture: teenage suicides in Arkansas, video selling-power on television, and Archie and his friends in Riverdale, no longer the innocents we once knew, but jaded individuals who have been marauded of their decency.

What else do we have? We have a counterculture. We have Jesus. And what a contrast he offers his followers. The culture comes to steal and kill. He comes as counterculture and to give life—and to give it most abundantly.

15

+

New Year's Resolutions

Matthew 3:13–17

On New Year's Day our thoughts turn to resolutions. To keep up with tradition, I want to suggest three New Year's resolutions. But before I do, I want to establish the context of the resolutions and the context comes from a fine article in the *New York Times*, on the op-ed page; it's by John Wheeler, who is the president of the Center for the Viet Nam Generation. What he has to say is interesting.

His main theme is that there will be a great rebirth of faith in the 1990s. And this, he says, is due to the demographic changes. There are sixty million in the Viet Nam generation, the so-called baby boomers—and they are rethinking a lot of things.

He says, for example: "In a survey of eight hundred 'baby boomers,' the Center for the Viet Nam Generation found that 69% believed in God or a positive, active, spiritual force; and 40% reported that they had become more spiritual in the past five years." This is the baby boomer generation, supposed to be turned in and very self-centered, and yet faith is markedly increasing. We can even see that in our faith communities: in the large number of young people who are raising children and who are worshiping with us. There is a measurable return.

Well, this man John Wheeler gives three reasons for this re-kindling of faith. First, he says, "The United States is in a season of remembrance." He points out that all over the country there are memorials going up, such as the Viet Nam Memorial in Washington, D.C. He points out that there are 143 major Viet Nam memorials, and makes an interesting comment. He says, "Memorials awaken questions of faith. 'Are there things worth dying for? Is death the last word?'" He's right. Every memorial that you put up implicitly asks those two questions. Is there something worth dying for? Is death the last word? And they ask one more question: What are we remembering?

The second reason he gives for the awakening of faith in the baby boom generation is "the affirmation of fundamental values. This is a rocky time for many, and given the size of our age group, more than sixty million, it will be a rocky time for the country in general. For many, the reevaluation and affirmation of faith happen because life awakens us to the spiritual void caused by fixation on money and material possessions, by marital infidelity, and by self-concern."

And he continues: "Science is the third force that needs our faith. Stephen Hawking and Carl Sagan personify it. Their exploration of the universe makes recourse, as in Genesis, to metaphor and to simile, to great figures of speech that bespeak a profound mystery about life."

He's backed up by the polls, which say that 54 percent of adults think that religion is very important, and 31 percent think that it's fairly important, which means that 85 percent feel that, indeed, religion and faith in God are important. So he's right. People are reacting to the void, to the materialism, to some of the horrors of the past couple of decades, horrors spawned in the 1960s and 1970s: the drug culture, the divorce culture. All these things have so much brokenness to them. They're saying there's got to be a return to faith in God.

So in view of these three things and in view of the high incidence of faith, I suggest three simple New Year's resolutions, for what they're worth. And you can let them rinse over you, and accept or reject them, as you might.

The first is to reconsider your call. There's a lovely meditation by the great Jesuit spiritual writer Anthony deMello. He
asks us to use our imaginations and to go back and meet St.
Peter, and he says:

> I imagine I am present when Jesus first meets Peter and
> pronounces him a rock. I am standing by the lakeside
> when he inspires Peter, Andrew, James, and John to catch
> human beings. I visit Peter in his cell before his execution.
> He looks back on the day when Jesus called him, and the
> things he saw and learned and felt. The kind of work, the
> kind of life he would have had if Jesus had not met him.
>
> I look back, too, on the day when Jesus called me, just
> as Peter does. Then Peter shares his feelings at the
> thought that he must die tomorrow. "This call is still
> alive. Each day it talks to me—I do not know what. What
> was I called to yesterday?" The voice that spoke to the Fa-
> ther, the voice that spoke to Mary, the voice that spoke to
> Peter, is the voice that speaks to me. I know not what it
> calls me to, but I recognize the voice and I give it my re-
> sponse.

Reconsider your call. Why do you go to church? Seriously,
why? Why are you called? What difference does it mean to
you to be a Catholic? To answer that question look beyond the
externals you read about in the press: the travels of the pope,
the disputes among bishops and in the synods, the Vatican
comings and goings, the money, the scandals. They're irrelevant. What really counts is that Jesus Christ calls us to this tradition. We are still reading the same scripture that was read
two thousand years ago.

Now someone might say: "Well, that just proves you're in a
rut." But on the other hand it proves that we stand in an in-
credibly long tradition. We are breaking the same bread and
we are sharing the same cup that have been broken and shared
for two thousands years, uninterruptedly. You stand in a long
line of basic Catholic Christianity that goes back to Christ

himself in the time of the apostles. You have been called in baptism, so I just suggest that maybe one New Year's resolution is to reconsider your call. Feel good about being a Catholic. Feel proud about who and what you are, about being a part of a two-thousand-year tradition centered in the word of God and the breaking of the bread. Reconsider your call. What's God calling you to? What does God want from you in the coming year?

The second resolution is this: Pick up on what others have started. Some of you have known losses. You've lost spouses, you've lost children, you've lost relationships, you've lost health, you've lost equilibrium. You name it—there are losses scattered all over the landscape. But you have your choice about these losses. Your choice is either to turn in on yourself and forever cry "woe is me," or you can pick up on those who turn tragedy into discipleship.

I think, for example, of that little Japanese girl who you've heard about, Sadaku. She was one of those kids who was caught in the bombing of Hiroshima, and she saw her mother and father and her family destroyed before her; and she herself had severe radiation burns. She was in a hospital and, fundamentally, was waiting to die, and she knew she didn't have long. But instead of bemoaning the tragedy, she said: "This can never happen again to people. People can't be this cruel to one another. So each day I'm going to cut out and make a white crane, and I'm going to send it to somebody and ask them to be a disciple for peace." Well, she did that every day for 683 days, and then she died.

And those who knew this little girl had their choice. They could be so outraged over the bombings that they'd be consumed by a desire to go out and bomb the rest of the world in revenge, or they could pick up on what she started—and they did. And so they made a 684th white crane, and a 685th, and they go on *ad infinitum*, and those white cranes go throughout the world saying that life can be better.

Build on the people you know and on the people you don't know. Think, and do something with MADD (Mothers

Against Drunk Driving), something to help a mother or father who has lost a child because of someone's drunkenness. Instead of getting angry and blowing up the world, organizations like that are trying to make the world better. This is what I mean. Do something to make life better: say "no" to drugs, say "no" to sexual promiscuity. Make a resolution like that instead of bemoaning all that's terrible in the world.

There are homeless people to house, there are hungry people to feed. There are cranes to be cut out and sent. And it's a good resolution, isn't it? Pick up on what others have done. Continue the decent people's love and spirit which will turn the world around.

The third resolution is this: Show someone this year what God is like. I came up with that because a man was telling me a story. When he was a little boy he was forever coming home late from school. His parents were fed up with it because he came in late for dinner every day. So they finally got fed up and said, "Look, next time you come late for dinner, you're getting bread and water. That's it!"

So sure enough, the next day he came late for dinner, and he walked into the house and there were his mother and father, and they had plates with meat and potatoes and vegetables and all that good stuff—and in front of him were a plate of bread and a glass of water. He was crushed, he said.

The father waited for the full weight of the lesson to sink in, and then silently the father took his full plate and put it in front of his son, and he took his son's empty plate and put it in front of himself. And this man, the boy who is now a man, said to me last week, "All my life I have known what God is like by what my father did that night." It's as simple as that.

People learn about God not because they figure out the Trinity, not because they tune into Vatican doings, not because they're great theologians, not because they understand Greek. People learn about God from Godlike people. Even people who have done evil in their lives, even people who have messy corners they're dealing with. You can still share a full plate with someone who has none, so to speak. You can be God to some people who will remember what God is like because they remember what you did.

So those are my three suggested New Year's resolutions. Reconsider your call. You wouldn't be a part of a church if you weren't called. For all of our individual and collective failings, there is a beauty of God's holy church—the church of Jesus Christ—still nurtured by word and sacrament. Reconsider your call. Be proud of it. Pick up what others have started— you can make a difference. And show somebody this year what God is like. If we half keep these three resolutions, then indeed the coming year will be a very happy new year.

16

+

Five Things Prayer Is Not

Matthew 6:7–15

My topic is prayer, and I'm going to come at it from a different angle, from the negative perspective, if you will. Or, to put it another way, I want to share, through reflection and story, five things prayer is not. That may help us at some other time to discover what prayer *is*.

The first is that prayer is not just saying prayers. That means that prayer without a context of justice and charity is false. Jesus reserved some of his harshest words for people who just said prayers. "Beware of the scribes. These are the ones who swallow up the property of widows while making a show of lengthy prayers. When you pray do not imitate such hypocrites."

So, therefore, prayer is not a matter of saying prayers. Rather, prayer is primarily a lived context in which our prayers are finally said.

A busload of teenagers was returning from Mexico. They had gone down there as a kind of Christian charity to help out the exceedingly poor people. They had worked hard all day and they got back into the bus; they were very tired, and they were very, very hungry. They crossed the border back into the

United States and they stopped at a diner; and they waited. And it seemed they waited a long time, and finally one of them got bold enough to go over to the waitress and ask if they could be served. The waitress told them she would serve them, but they (indicating the two black teenagers among them) would have to eat in the bus. The teenagers looked at one another, and one of them finally said, "Well, we weren't hungry, anyway," and they went back to the bus.

Two people got up the next morning to pray. One was the waitress and one was one of the teenagers. Who just said prayers and who really prayed? It's the very thing that the gospel before us says: "Not everybody who says to me, 'Lord, Lord,' shall enter the kingdom of heaven, but the one who does the will of my heavenly Father."

Prayer is not just saying prayers. Prayer flows out of, and is a part of, a context of justice and charity. Again, Jesus was very clear on this. If you are on your way to church to offer your gift at the altar and remember that your brother has something against you, leave your gift at the altar and go be reconciled to your brother, and then come back and make your offering. So prayer is not just saying prayers. That's the first point.

Second, prayer, contrary to popular notion, is not a matter of withdrawing from one's culture. We have a kind of heritage of that. If we want to pray, or be a genuine pray-er, or be a man or woman of prayer, then we think we just have to leave society and go off into the desert for about forty or fifty years; then that's really prayer. And I think the reason that we think that way is because we have a misinterpretation, and a little bit of Hollywood imagery in our minds. Our model of prayer is an idealized image of the monastic life. And our vision of prayer is that in the old days the monks went out into the hinterlands and into the monasteries, and they spent the days in prayer.

The historical reality is quite the opposite. The monks were at the height of life. In medieval times the monks were in the thick of political power. Those of you who know your history will realize how many popes came from the monastery. The monks were at the center of economic power. They owned the large farms. They ran the farms. They were at the heart and soul of the economic life of their times. The monks were at the heart of education. Where else could people go to read and write except the monasteries? And the monks were at the heart of artistic creativity, as the manuscripts, the stained-glass windows, and those marvelous illuminations show us.

So what I'm saying here is that the reason the monks were such good pray-ers is not because they withdrew from their culture, but on the contrary, they were good pray-ers because they were deeply within their culture. And therefore our own ideal of prayer doesn't fit the historical reality. Prayer is not withdrawing from one's culture. If prayer were solely a personal matter, we'd say "My Father..." instead of "Our Father...." We'd use the singular instead of the plural.

But it is "*Our* Father," *our* life, *our* society, *our* culture, *our* time, *our* place; and it is in community, in our culture, that we will be pray-ers. And if we will not be pray-ers in our culture, we won't be pray-ers on the mountain top.

Third, prayer is not causing God to change by our petitions. That's a hard one to think about. Our prayer is not designed to change God's mind. A child lives in the world of petitions: "I want, I need, and you provide."

But for adults prayer is rather recalling the presence of God, and opening ourselves to that. You are not out to change God's mind, you are out to be changed.

A mother of several young children was having a very difficult time dealing with one of her sons, who was really being treated rather unfairly and unjustly at school. She agonized for days over what she might do about the problem. Should she step in? Or maybe it would be best if she kept her hands off and let the kid work it out by himself. She decided on the second option, and then she had second thoughts, and she was worried because he was a sensitive boy. Well, the problem haunted her for days and she couldn't sleep.

Finally one day she got in her car and she just drove out into the country. She pulled off to the side of the road, and she laid her head on the steering wheel, and she cried, and she cried, and she cried. And when she was all cried out, she lifted her head and looked out in wonder at the great golden wheat field beside the road where she had parked. At first she was overcome by the sheer beauty of that golden scene, the wheat waving and dancing in the wind.

Then suddenly she realized there was something more to it, and she said (and I quote her words): "I knew what God was saying to me in that wheat field. And so I dried my eyes and I let its glories pour into me. I began to experience God's love. God didn't send me any easy solution to my problem, just the assurance of his knowing and caring, and that was enough because I knew that the same fatherly love would reach down and touch my hurting child."

So prayer is not a matter of being out to change God's mind. Prayer is primarily a matter of opening ourselves to a God who's there loving us all the time, and we just don't know it.

The fourth thing about prayer is that it is not primarily talking to God. This reminds me of the story of the little boy and his brother who went to visit their grandma; as the little boy said his night prayers he was shouting at the top of his voice, "Please God, send me a bicycle, send me a tool chest," and all that.

And his brother said, "Not so loud. For crying out loud, God isn't deaf."

And he said, "Yeah, I know, but grandma is."

But prayer isn't like that, you see. Prayer is rather trying to discern God's presence. Otherwise, you get people saying, "Well, you know, I prayed for hours and I received no answer, and no word from God."

But as a matter of fact, God has put God's Word in history and in life, and we have to be attuned to where it is. Prayer is not talking to God. That's not a good definition. Prayer is listening to God.

A man and his family were in a motel room. He was to give a speech at a convention. The program was extremely precise. He had only "x" number of minutes to give that speech and therefore it was important for him to have the correct time, and he was going out of his mind because he had misplaced his watch. Well, his wife and the kids were running all over the room looking for it and he was in a panic because time was growing short, and suddenly he shouted at the top of his voice, "Everybody freeze!" And everybody just stopped where they were. Total silence—till they heard the ticking. And in the silence they found the watch.

Prayer is like that. Prayer is not talking to God, it's listening. But you have to quiet down, and you have to be silent, and you'll hear what's there.

Fifth and last, prayer, contrary to popular mythology, is not an exceptional experience, a mystical experience for the elite, for the saints. Some people do, in fact, have mystical experiences, but that's not the whole of prayer. That's like saying baseball is sports. Yes, baseball is a part of sports, but it's not all sports. So mystical experiences and exceptional experiences are not prayer; if you believe that they are prayer, then you make prayer an experience for the elite and you come to feel that if you haven't been slain by the Spirit, or heard voices, or seen visions, then prayer is not for you, and you are simply out of the ballpark. But prayer is for everyone. It's not a special thing for some.

The mother mouse knew that sooner or later she'd have to introduce her little mice to the real world, so the day came when she said, "Children, come with me. We're venturing outside."

So they all gathered around Mamma Mouse, and they poked their heads through the mouse hole and walked outside. Right there was a big, black, sleeping cat. Mamma Mouse's heart was throbbing, but she decided these kids had to learn about life sooner or later, so she tiptoed with her brood around the sleeping cat, who suddenly opened one eye, and raised his paw. Mamma Mouse arched her back, let out two heavy barks, and the cat went scampering out of the room. She turned to her children and said, "Children, I want you to know that when you get into a tight spot, it always helps to have a second language."

Well, that refers to what I'm saying here: people feel that prayer is a second language for the knowledgeable, the clever, and the elite who have studied that second language. But my contention is that prayer is not an exceptional experience for the clever; prayer is an ordinary experience for the likes of you and me, and—as for those mice—it's an essential part of life and of maturing.

Maybe I can summarize these five negative points in a story that happened about twenty years ago. A woman had called me because her non-Catholic husband had died, and in those days they would not bury him in a Catholic cemetery. It was in December. We had about three feet of snow. So I agreed to meet her and her daughter at the cemetery. I got to the cemetery and met her and her daughter, and she said, "I appreciate your coming, Father, and I would like to say a prayer for my husband. He's right over here."

Well, we walked down the row, in three or four feet of snow, and he wasn't there. So she said, "Well, I think he's over here," and we walked further and couldn't find him. And the daughter said, "No, Mommy, he's over here," and we walked there, and he wasn't there, either. We were freezing, and my feet were getting colder, and the mother says, "No, I think he's over here," and he wasn't there either.

And finally, I saw her face grow stern. I could see she was angry at him once more—mad as a hatter. She said, "George, where the hell are you?" I put my face in my ritual, the daughter broke up, and then finally the mother laughed. The two of them embraced each other and laughed; and after the laughter stopped, then they cried. After the crying stopped, we all said a prayer for George, wherever he was.

And that about sums up my five points. Prayer is not just saying prayers; it's living a life of charity. So we were there in charity, in a cold winter. We were doing something; we were not just saying words.

Second, prayer is not withdrawing from the world. No, we were there in the rhythms of life and death, and all the things that make up your life and mine.

Third, prayer is not causing God to change. We weren't trying to bring George back. Rather prayer causes us to change and to live through the mysteries and the redemptive love of Jesus' death.

Fourth, prayer is not talking to God, but listening, trying to discern and listen to God's voice even in the midst of tragedy.

And fifth, prayer is not an exceptional experience for the mystic. In that cemetery we were three ordinary people who laughed and cried in the same five minutes.

So maybe these negative points clear the ground for what prayer is not. And knowing what it is not, we may be ready for the glory and the beauty of what prayer is.

17

✛

Between Loss and Promise

Acts 1:1–14

A part of this reading says: "After Jesus was taken up into the heavens the apostles returned to Jerusalem, a mere Sabbath's Day away, and entering the city, they went to the upstairs room where they were staying."

You read between the lines. It's not hard to do. Luke is giving us a very common theme that speaks to us today. He's saying, "Look, this is a shattered community. They have lost their leader. And not only lost him, but lost him most shamefully, because their leader was roughly grabbed and given a criminal's death."

And so they don't know what to do. They remember some words of Jesus and they go to this upper room to figure things out, and to hope that his words might be true and that something might happen. But for the moment you have to appreciate that they are in the "in-between time." They're between the Ascension and Pentecost—between loss and promise.

And the scriptures show us how they handled that, and that's important because all of us at one time or another are exactly there—between loss and promise, between things that you have lost and things that have not yet unfolded, and you're in that limbo of "in-between time."

An example is when someone close to you dies. You are in a vacuum. And the pain of the loss is there, and the future doesn't seem to be anywhere, and you're in between.

Those going away to school for the first time—going away to college. You don't know the place or the kids well enough; you don't know your way around. And there's the security of home and the insecurity of the college; and homesickness sets in. You are in the "in-between time." Between pain and promise.

Those of you who have lost your jobs, you know what being in between means. You can be vice-president of a company one day and lose your job the next day. And all of a sudden all those things that were important are stripped away, and you don't yet have a new job.

And perhaps worst of all—even worse than death in many ways—is suffering through broken relationships, whether it's a divorce, or the break-up of a friendship, or estrangement from a child who's living a life that you don't like—living in disgrace and sin, living through addictions or prison.

So you see this "in-between time" of the apostles is something that you and I know from our experience. Will I ever get better? Will this mental or emotional or physical illness ever leave me? Will I ever be free? We all know those questions.

The scripture suggests three things to do, the things the apostles did.

The first thing they did was to gather in prayer. They just didn't know what to do except that they had to pray for guidance, even when it was difficult to pray. And I imagine that it had to be. All they knew was that their leader was dead. He had promised the Spirit, and the Spirit had not yet come. They didn't know whether they had a future as a sect or a religion, or whether they should just split up and go back into the mainstream. And even though they were not inclined to, they prayed. So that's the first thing that Luke, who wrote this story, gives us on how to handle the "in-between times."

The second thing is interesting. Luke implies: "Look for and savor the message of simplicity."

What does he mean by that? He means that when you have

loss, things are stripped from you. If you lost your job, your name on the door is stripped from you. Your conversation, your social circle, is contracted. It's not something that you talk about at a cocktail party. Suddenly your connections are gone, and so is the daily routine of going to work. You're without many of the people who know you and respect you. Suddenly you're without identity. It's that kind of thing. Things are being stripped from you.

Sickness strips the ability to come and go as you will. Broken relationships, a divorce, physical or mental illness—all these losses ultimately strip you. And Luke says that when things are stripped away, as bad as that is, it has a tendency to force you to go down to the bare-bones values of your life. You and I have read stories about people and know people who have met great tragedies that in the end helped them to focus on what really counted. You are divested of your cumbersome symbols; and hopefully, being stripped this way and having to live more simply, you realign your values. Maybe the best thing to do is to look at those people who voluntarily strip themselves. They don't have to do it.

I think of one of the bishops in a diocese of Brazil, Bishop Pedro. When he was consecrated, he would not wear the usual mitre and the rings, and wouldn't carry the crozier. Instead, he said, "My mitre will be the straw sombrero of the poor. My ring will be works of mercy, and my staff will be service to the people."

Stripping down his life to bare essentials. He could live in a castle, and he would live in great honor, but voluntarily he chose to live close to the values that really count: people and relationships, and loving one another.

Or if you don't want to talk about a bishop, talk about a tennis star. I was much impressed by Boris Becker of West Germany, who twice won the Wimbleton tennis tournament. He suddenly realized that he was becoming more than a famous world tennis champion. He suddenly realized that Germany was making him a source of its new pride, and he found himself being idolized. And that is very seductive—whether you're fifty-nine or twenty-nine, much less nineteen. But for his young age, he said this, and I quote: "The Germans wanted me to live for them. They worship too much. When I entered my own home town people stood there and gazed up at me as if they were expecting blessings from the pope. When I looked into the eyes of my fans at the Davis Cup matches last December, I thought I was looking at monsters. Their eyes were fixed and had no life in them. When I saw this kind of blind, emotional devotion, I could understand what happened to us a long time ago at Nuremberg." (Here he was making a reference to when Hitler mesmerized the German people.) And then he said: "Heroes live very short lives."

So he stripped himself of all those honors and stepped back from that kind of adulation and the kind of personality cult that you read about in *People* magazine. He wanted to be authentically himself.

So in this stripping away time, you are forced to say, "What are the values I really want to live by?"

And when the apostles went to that upper room they had to ask that question: "What are we basically, when all is taken away—you take away my house, my car, my income, my health, what really counts?"

The "in-between time" is a graceful moment for answering that question.

And the third thing is to live in the seedtime of hope. Jesus had said: "If you go there, the Spirit will come upon you."

Was that true or not? They didn't want to believe it and yet there was that tantalizing hope. They were tantalized by a hope for renewal and surprise. For example, we are all delighted that Mathias Rust took his little Cessna airplane and flew into Red Square.[1]

But you see the thing that we're so delighted about is that this is a surprise of the Spirit. Moscow has antiballistic missiles to defend it, and all kinds of sophisticated radar, and the Mos-

---

1 On May 29, 1987, Mathias Rust, a nineteen-year-old German, flew a single-engine Cessna from Helsinki to Red Square. His flight went undetected by Soviet air defenses. He embarrassed the heck out of the Soviets, so much so that they fired many people in the military. Gorbachev wanted to do that anyway. (My guess is that he hired Mathias, but that's only a personal theory.)

covites didn't dream that something like this could or would happen—and then a nineteen-year-old German flies undetected and lands there. Surprise of the Spirit. And if you look at the photographs of Red Square, where does he land? In front of the great cathedral of St. Basil, that magnificent building. It has been turned into a museum of atheism by the Soviets. But it stands there, and religion is flourishing in the Soviet Union as never before. Try as they might to kill God, God keeps popping out in the most unexpected places. So it's significant that the plane landed in front of St. Basil's because that stands not as the official museum to atheism, it stands as a symbol of unexpected hope for the deeply religious Russian people.

Let me tell you another true story. Most of you at least know the name of Edwin Booth. Back in 1865, Edwin Booth was the Laurence Olivier of the stage. Actually one of the greatest dramatic actors the world has ever seen. But he had a horrible life, and he lived under a cloud. He lived in the "in-between time" for a long time.

He had a terrible father. His father, Brutus Booth, was a drunk and drank himself to death. He stranded his family 3000 miles away in California, and they had to work back to their native Maryland. The only way that Edwin knew how was by becoming an actor.

His first wife, Mary Devlin, died after two years of marriage. Talk about a soap opera, one thing after another. He remarried and his other wife became insane, and he went bankrupt trying to pay for her medication. What else could happen to him?

What else happened was something that embarrassed him his whole life long—his own younger brother assassinated President Lincoln. John Wilkes Booth was Edwin's younger brother.

Edwin was a pro-Union, pro-Lincoln patriot, so not only did it offend him that way, but this was his brother. And everybody knows what it means to have a member of your family embarrass you, which is a great understatement. After all, his brother killed the president of the United States, one of our greatest.

And for a long time, in that seedtime, in that "in-between time," he did the best thing that he could in order to compensate. He became that great actor. But the Spirit surprised him one day.

He was in Jersey City, and there was a tall young man there being pushed by a crowd, nudged to such an extent that the young man started to fall onto the railroad tracks. Edwin Booth, who happened to be there, dropped his valise and immediately ran over, and just in the nick of time literally snatched this young man from death. The young man recognized the famous actor from his photographs and simply said, "Well, that was a narrow escape, Mr. Booth."

And for as long as he lived, Edwin Booth took pleasure in the knowledge that the person whose life he saved was Robert Todd Lincoln, President Lincoln's eldest son. So the Spirit came when he least expected it to give him a sense of decency again.

So it looks like a little, harmless story that Luke is telling, but he's saying that the time between the loss and the promise is hard, but the scripture has left us a program for the "in between time."

You must pray. You must pray even when the prayer that you make is "I can't pray." You must pray in faith even when the content of your prayer is "I can't believe and I don't think you exist at all." You must pray to a higher power. The "in-between time" is difficult, a transition in your life.

Second, you must look for the value-message in the stripping away. Every loss forces you into looking at things. People know that, especially those who visit hospitals. In hospitals I've heard more than one person say, "If I had to do it all over again, I would spend more time with my spouse. I would listen to my children more. We would spend more time together. I would appreciate each day in this world, and look at the flowers more," and so forth and so on. When you're stripped away and you're faced with essentials of life and death, there's a great grace there. So in the "in-between times" you must sit back and look for the calling mystery of your new-found simplicity that will help you to realign your values, so you can be a good human being.

And third, it's a "seedtime of hope." The word "seed" is good, for those of you who putter in gardens. You drop the seed in the ground, and you can look every day as the kids do, and nothing's happening. But something is happening. Unknown, invisibly, something incredible is happening, something you could watch with time-lapse photography. What's happening is that the seed is dying. But in the very process of dying, as it must die, the shoot comes forth. That's hope.

So those of you who are in the "in-between time," or will be, and everybody will be—just be patient with the dying, but have hope for the future.

The Spirit that entered Edwin Booth's life and the unexpected landing in Red Square are positive signs that the Spirit will breathe where it will, and therefore, in the "in-between time," we have a right to hope.

18

+

Jesus, Collector of the Unwanted: All Saints Day

Revelation 7:14–17

At St. Mary's we have a long-standing and perhaps strange custom: at Mass on Halloween morning people wear their costumes. And were you to walk in a little bit late and come in the front door of the church, scattered all around would be assorted ghouls and ghosts and skeletons and monsters. And indeed, you would wonder if you had stumbled into a Catholic church or Greenwich Village.

Some would be scandalized at that, feeling that it is somewhat irreverent for adults to be dressing up like children and coming to church in their costumes and masks. And yet I would share with you on this Feast of All Saints that, in fact, what they are doing is based very solidly on the scripture that we have before us.

Chapter 7 of the Book of Revelation opens up with a great vision of John the Apostle. He sees all those who have been saved, and he says the total number is 144,000—twelve thou-

sand from every one of the twelve tribes of Judah. And a few
verses down, he lists the tribes: twelve thousand from the tribe
of Asher; twelve thousand from the tribe of Benjamin; and so
he goes.

And you ask what's the meaning of these numbers? The
meaning is that for the ancients numbers were not mathemat-
ics—numbers were symbols. They meant something very
deep. And the favorite numbers of the ancients were pretty
much like ours. We've inherited that. The number three, the
number seven, and the number twelve. Twelve tribes of Israel,
twelve apostles, twelve pillars of wisdom, and so it goes. And
therefore, when the scripture says that there were 144,000 who
were saved, it is saying something very symbolic. One hundred and forty-four is twelve times twelve, and twelve is the
number of perfection, and those who are saved are twelve
times perfection, if you can imagine that. Twelve to the infinite
exponent, if you will.

And as soon as you begin to understand that, you begin to
understand the shift. And the shift is not to all the saints who
are saved, this vast 144,000; the shift is to the mercy of God.
The Feast of All Saints is a celebration of God. It says that these
144,000 from every tribe—the strangest people are numbered
among them—are a tribute to the fact that where we would
draw lines, God doesn't. Where we would have included a
very select few to be saved, God seems to be very prodigal.
Where we would have rejected others, God seems to have accepted them. Where we would have dwindled the numbers,
God has expanded them to 144,000 people of every tongue and
language and way of life, has included them in these vast
numbers. How great God must be. How splendidly merciful.
How generous.

And you see, you take that back a step further, and what
you have very profoundly and simply is the gospel. What is
our gospel that brings us together? We believe in Jesus Christ;
and Jesus Christ is the revelation of the Father; and Jesus
Christ would not draw the lines that we would draw. What do
we know about Jesus? That he hung around with marginal

people. The people we would exclude, he included. It is Jesus who cured the daughter of the Syro-Phoenician woman although she was a foreigner, and in those days people did not care about those beyond their borders.

It was Jesus who cured the servant of the Roman centurion even though he was of a hated, occupying force. We would have dismissed this Roman. He had pity where we would not have pity. The lepers had to walk on the other side of the street and wear a bell to clear the place so that nobody would touch them, but Jesus allowed them to come to him; he touched the lepers and cured them when no one else would go near them, and one came back and thanked him.

It is Jesus who called Levi, the hated publican and quisling, who was collecting taxes for the occupation forces, and changed his name to Matthew and said, "Come, follow me." It is Jesus who told the story of the woman who swept her house for a single penny. It is Jesus who told the irrational story of a shepherd who left ninety-nine and went to look for the one. It is Jesus who let the scarlet woman touch him when we would have withdrawn our feet. When Jesus went through Samaritan territory, and they refused him, the disciples asked him to cast down fire on them, and he said, "No, let's go another way. This is not the way I work."

So what we have on this Feast of All Saints is the fact that God is much more generous than we would ever imagine; that God is much more inclusive than we could ever think; that in Jesus Christ, God is more accepting and welcoming than we would ever dream—it was Jesus who hung around with the marginal and those outside the Law, the deformed, the ugly, the unbeautiful, the scarred.

And that was the message yesterday morning when all of these adults came here with their faces grotesque and monstrous and deformed and hurt. They were sitting here as representations of all the ugliness and sinfulness and hurtfulness and brokenness that people are capable of. They were here with their monster masks and their distorted limbs and their ugliness as if to say every one is repulsed but Jesus. They were here in their costumes as a paean to the gospel that says that each one of us, some way or another, is disfigured and imperfect and flawed; and the only one who looks at our ugliness and sees beauty is Jesus.

When others would exclude us, when others would reject us, when others would not invite us to their parties, Jesus does. When others shun us and turn their backs and reject us and hurt us, Jesus breaks bread with us. When others look at our appearance and are repulsed, Jesus kisses us.

So, each Halloween when people here dress in costumes and masks it is a celebration in action. You have a gospel in action. You have a representation of the 144,000, the endless number that God includes, but which we probably would exclude. That's why I say the Feast of All Saints is God's feast. A feast of someone who possibly could love me. A feast of someone who would look behind the ugliness of my mask, and sinfulness, and pain, and hurt, someone who would look at my physical and moral ills and still love me.

This is the celebration of one who will include vast numbers of those who are outside the law, beyond the borders, and without any redeeming features. This is the God of ghosts and ghouls, and goblins and witches, and brokenness. One hundred and forty-four thousand, twelve times twelve, endless, infinite mercy is what this feast is all about.

Or, to put it simply, it's about Jesus, who said, "Come to me, all of you who are labored and are ugly and are burdened, and I will refresh you; for my burden is easy and my yoke is light."

19

+

Responding to Evil

Matthew 13:24–43

In its own way this is an enormously profound gospel and parable because what it's dealing with is one of the great mysteries of life. When we say a mystery it means that we simply don't have answers to it. And that major mystery is the mystery of evil. Where did it come from and why does it exists? And why doesn't God do something about it?

In this parable we have the figure of speech of good seed being sown and all of a sudden this evil weed is coming up and choking it to death. The only kind of so-called answer Jesus gives us is that at judgment time things will be evened out, but meantime you live with ambiguity and let the weeds and the wheat, the good and the evil, grow up together.

But there's also something else in this parable, and not only in the parable but in the way Jesus lived his life. You say, O.K., we have incredible evil. Why is this allowed? Why do people abuse children? Why are they selling drugs to teenagers? Why are they hurting one another? These babies you read about, born with AIDS, living at most three years. Why do these innocent little babies have to suffer for the activity of their parents? How do we live in a world of evil? And evil there is.

And Jesus seems to say, and to portray in the way he lived, this:

"Look, there's not an answer, but there's a way that you must act."

And the best way I can describe this is just to share with you some little stories, and they may better give the approach than any other way.

Last week I was with a fellow priest and at different times, like everybody else, we'd talk shop. And he happened to have with him a letter he had gotten the previous week. It's an interesting letter because the letter was to the pastor but it was addressed to "Harry, the usher." And the letter, which I got a copy of, goes like this:

Dear Harry:

I'm sorry I don't know your last name, but then you don't know mine. You're at the ten o'clock Mass each Sunday. I'm writing to ask a favor. I don't know the priest too well, but somehow I feel close to you. I don't know how you got to know my first name, but every Sunday morning you smile and greet me by name, and we exchange a few words: how bad the weather is, how much you like my hat, and how I was late on a particular Sunday.

I just wanted to say thank you for taking the time for remembering an old lady, for the smiles, for your consideration, for your thoughtfulness. Now for my favor.

I am dying, Harry. My husband has been dead for sixteen years and the kids are scattered. It is very important to me when they bring me to church for the last time that you will be standing there in the front entrance. It wouldn't seem right if you didn't say, "Hello, Gert. Good to see you."

If you are there, Harry, I feel assured that your warm hospitality will be duplicated in my new home in heaven.

With love and gratitude,
Gert

You are familiar with Charles Kuralt, who has that "On the Road" series. Sometimes I get that on television, and he also writes a column called "On the Road." In traveling all over, up and down the United States, he came to some conclusions a few years ago, and I share his words:

I've been told that during the Reagan years America has turned inward, that is, people have become selfish. I keep reading this, but I see mighty little evidence of this. I have found a lot to be confident and reassured about. More decency and compassion and public spirit. Less greed and arrogance and hostility. I don't think change in America has much to do with whoever is in the White House or which party controls the Congress. Even in a complex, technological society, it turns out it is one man or one woman with an idea that touches the national consciousness.

A Rachel Carson, or a Ralph Nader, or Martin Luther King, Jr. A woman who says no, she believes she will not move to the back of the bus today as the law requires, because she's tired from her work and tired of that law. And soon, not without pain, everything changes. These ideas don't originate from Washington. They spring from the land, which is the way it was supposed to work in the first place.

And then there's the Geis family, Miep and Heinrich. She worked for Otto Frank. In 1933 when the Nazis came in, she hid the Frank family up in the secret room in the attic, as you know. She was the one who every day brought food and news up to the Frank family. She was the one who gave Anne Frank her first and last pair of high heel shoes. She was the one who recovered the diary after they had been killed.

She wrote a book called *Anne Frank Remembered*. And she simply says, "We did nothing unusual, we Dutch people. We were very ordinary people."

But she said, "You know, during the occupation there were

just two kinds of people—those who collaborated and those who resisted."

I have a doctor friend who on several days during the year goes upstairs to his closet and he takes out of it a coat that is out of style, one sleeve is patched, and it's rather tawdry and stringy and dirty. He showed it to me one day and I asked him why he wore it on certain days of the year.

And he told me that once when he was an intern in New York City, in lower Manhattan, he got a call one very blustery, cold, wintry night. A little girl came banging at his door. He threw on his jacket and he went over to a stinking tenement, up very dirty stairs into a little one-room apartment where a little boy was lying terribly sick, hovered over by his mother and father. He did what he could for the malnourished child, but in spite of his best efforts the little boy died then and there in front of him.

He was shivering not only from the hurt of the boy dying, but because there was no heat in that tenement. And the boy's father took off his coat, this very coat, and gave it to him and said, "Here, you're cold. Thank you for trying to save our boy."

The doctor knew then and there that that was the only way that this couple could possibly thank him. He didn't have the heart to refuse or turn it back. And now that he's prominent and fairly wealthy, once or twice a year—on the anniversary of that boy's death, and the day that he got his diploma to be a doctor—to remind himself what it's all about, he wears that coat.

And finally, we have the *Man of La Mancha*, based on Cervantes's story of Don Quixote, who doesn't really have a full deck; he runs around tilting at windmills and doing ridiculous stuff; he adores a woman named Aldonza, who is a horror, and a mess, and a wimp of a woman, and calls her Dulcinea. Those of you who know languages can see the word "sweet" in there. He calls her "sweet one," which causes everybody in town to roar because Aldonza is anything but sweet. She's a tramp. She's a mess.

But you might recall that in spite of this Quixote loved her, as no one else had in her life before. And you might remember that as Quixote is dying and breathing his last, Aldonza sings a great song, "The Impossible Dream." You might remember that last scene. After she sings "The Impossible Dream," someone calls out her name, "Aldonza," and she lifts herself up from the dead Quixote, holds her head high, and says, "My name is Dulcinea."

The love of this man made her over.

So you see what Jesus says is there is no technical, direct answer to the problem and the mystery of all terrible evil in the world: poverty, torture, drugs, AIDS, you name it. How cruel we can be to one another. But the only thing Jesus does say is that in the end it will be all right, but meanwhile you make a difference where you can. That's the only response.

So you know what that means. That means that you and I are called upon to make a leap of faith. There's no common-sense way of dealing with evil. It doesn't respond to logic and common sense. And at times it's overwhelming. But the only response to this incredible evil is to really believe that you can make a difference and that your act of virtue can bring sun into the darkness. And that somehow it will count.

So we are asked to greet the lonely, like Harry, the usher. We are asked to make a difference, like America's little people, like Rosa Parks. We are asked to resist evil, like the Geises and the Frank family. We are asked to slip into the life of another with reverence, like my doctor friend. We are asked that when others use names that sting, degrade, or label, we use different names: names that are "sweeter."

In short, in this parable, the approach, if not the answer to evil, is always love.

20

✛

My Enemy, the Church

Matthew 5:38–48

You hear Jesus' words, "Let your light shine before others. Do not resist evil. If somebody strikes you on the right cheek, you're to turn and offer him the left."

If they ask for your shirt, you give the coat. If they press you for one mile, you're supposed to go two.

"Give to those who beg from you, and love your enemies, and pray for those who persecute you."

In a word, "we are to be perfect," Jesus says, "as the very God himself."

And when you hear words like this you just wonder how serious Jesus could be. In a Broadway play, a woman says, "God never made a better woman than I am, but somehow I just can't seem to live up to it."

And all those stories that we hear that are supposed to exemplify the ideal. The old story, for example, of the ancient Chinese warlord who ordered his general to go to a city and take the city and destroy all the enemies, no quarter, no nothing. About a week later the warlord went to the city and saw that the city gates were open, but when he went in he saw his general and the other soldiers having a banquet with all the natives there.

And furious, he asked about his order, about destroying the enemies, and of course the response was, "But I did. As you can see, they are now our friends."

Or there's the story about the man who once bought a farm and was walking the bounds of his new property when he met his new next-door neighbor.

And the new neighbor said to him, "Don't look now, but when you bought this piece of ground you also bought a lawsuit with it because your fence is ten feet on my property."

And the new owner smiled and said, "I thought I'd find some friendly neighbors here, and I'm going to. And you're going to help me. You move the fence over to where you want it and send me the bill, and we'll both be happy."

These are the kinds of stories that seem to translate this impossible dream of Jesus'. And still, on the other hand, in everyday flesh and blood life, beyond the stories, it is hard to love your enemy, particularly when you have been hurt deeply and, perhaps, in a most personal way.

Now imagine that your enemy is the church. Just think of all the headlines that have been in the papers the last few years. Think of what you've heard about the church on radio and television. The official church, what has it done to, say, Archbishop Hunthausen in Seattle?[1] Were they right? Were they wrong? Did they deal justly with him? Didn't they kind of defang him? Didn't they give his power to another, embarrassing them both?

Or you have the monsignor in St. Patrick's Cathedral who denied a wedding to a young man who has AIDS. Or you have the diocese of California which in preparation for the pope's visit decided to sell off television time, much to the horror of everybody because news is supposed to be unbiased and free, not sold.

You have those who may have been hurt by the laws on divorce and remarriage. Or the headline grabbers: John Paul v. Hans Küng, Charles Curran, in Washington, D.C., arm-

---

1 In September 1986, after Vatican inquiries into his positions on matters such as homosexuality and abortion, Archbishop Raymond Hunthausen of Seattle was directed to turn over some of his authority to an auxiliary bishop.

wrestling with Cardinal Ratzinger of the Vatican. This is the church that spawned Andy Greeley and Phil Donahue, Mother Teresa and, believe it or not, Madonna.

Or there are the news stories we hear about priests, stories that make some people angry or hostile. Any time you hear some gossip or bad news about a priest, then it is elevated to the entire Roman Catholic church.

I remember a story of Dorothy Day who had just attended Mass with a friend in New York. The priest was indeed a very poor liturgist. He had no sense of reverence, and his sermon was extraordinarily boring. It was just a terrible experience. On the way home the friend was wondering how Dorothy Day would react. After walking a bit in silence, Dorothy Day simply said, "If the church can survive priests like that, it just goes to prove that God must be with it."

I remember one of my own experiences in the last parish I was in (and you know how it is sometimes, those of you who teach or do any kind of public thing). This one Sunday everything that you could possibly imagine went wrong: the organist didn't show up, the lector was poor, the homily was terrible. The whole liturgy was a terrible disaster, just one of those bad days that we all have. And after the liturgy, as is the custom, I stood out in front of the church and hoped that I wouldn't get pillaged as the people went by. This one lady was known for her charity, and when I saw her coming, I said to myself, "If she says one nice thing about that liturgy, I'll know she's insincere." So she came up to me and shook my hand and she said, "Father, your vestments are beautiful."

So when we talk about the church being our enemy, we always tend to think of the pope and the bishops and the priests and even monsignors. But the fact is they are only a very insignificant and numerically small part of the church. Because after all, we are the church, all of us who are a part of it. And sometimes we give poor examples. Sometimes after looking at us and our behavior, people say: "Well, if that's what Catholicism is about, I want no part of it."

And yet, on the other hand, what we have to remember is

this: with all of our too human faults, which popes and priests
and every other member of God's church have, there is always
something more than meets the eye. In spite of family faults
(like our own families), there is a presence, and there is a reality, and there is a bonding, and there is love.

A professor of philosophy named William Shea wrote an article in *Commonweal*, in which he explains how he feels about
the Catholic church. He says:

> In addition to my feeling about the Church, I have a view
> of her. She is vital. She is gracefully engaged in the salva-
> tion of the world. Volatile, full of power for the Christian
> life. Promising, confident, confused, wrong-headed, stub-
> born, authoritarian, even perverse. But I am unable to
> make my affections for the church a distinction between
> the Catholic faith and the institutional church.
>
> As much as I now spontaneously dislike hierarchs and
> mistrust ecclesiastical bureaucrats, I think the distinction
> intellectually almost worthless and even a self-deception.
>
> Nor can I bring myself to say I love the church when
> her leaders are correct, and I do not love the church when
> they are mistaken.
>
> There is, to my mind, no institutional church of unfeel-
> ing bureaucrats, on the one side, and a nearly invisible
> church of good Catholics on the other. For me there's
> only one church. Right or wrong, sinful and saved, all at
> once. What you see is what you get, *per omnia saecula sae-
> culorum.*
>
> I am sad at her sins as I am at my own. I am wary of
> her penchant for intellectual and spiritual repression as I
> am of my own fear of power, and my primal resentment
> of criticism. I find writ large in her life my own struggle,
> my own good and evil, my own truth, and my own lie.

What I'm saying is that for all of the humanness and mistakes and even sinfulness of those of us who are the church,
we always have to have confidence that the bottom-line reality

is Jesus Christ. That he works his grace through us individually and collectively, imperfect and fractured as we are. There is a grace and there is a spirit that just are above us all.

Let me close by sharing with you a letter I got. The man's name is just Charles. I won't give you his last name. Apparently he came here on Christmas Eve, dropped in, and about a month later he sent me this letter. He says:

Dear Father Bausch:

Strange letter, but I'm an infidel, really Unitarian, who just happened to wander by your church on Christmas Evening at the request of a lonely Catholic widow who wished to pay her respects to God and her late-departed while being bolstered by some companionship en route. So I acted out the part, with doubts beforehand. You see, I had attended a Catholic Midnight Mass in my youth with another, younger lass, and had jumbled, rather distasteful memories of high ritual, babblings in Latin, great ceremony, and very little in which I felt the slightest understanding or empathy.

And then came Christmas Evening at St. Mary's with what was billed a "folk Mass," a very human and direct sermon by Father Bausch *sans* mumbo-jumbo, with several allusions that brought a smile to my face and an unexpected lump to my throat. A batch of kids and not-quite-kids singing carols and psalms with evident joy and an extraordinary degree of sincere professionalism, with guitars and such for the background instead of a ponderous but uninspiring organ. And even the responsive prayers were simple, understandable, all in English, and obviously felt from both the lectern and the congregation. Strange—very strange.

On the evening of Christmas, 1986, a cynic, a man with a good scientific education and a very dim view of the future of homo sapiens, felt a resurging of hope for the future of his children and a transient hope for the existence of a benign God, both snippets of wishful thinking effectively diminished by the front pages of the 1987 issues of *The New York Times,* as that venerable paper reported the mendacity of the leaders in government of the United States of America.

Although I don't believe (at least nowadays) in either God, or the so-called sanctity of my country, and therefore am undoubtedly an intellectual rogue, I want to thank you for that service and that hour. If there were many more of the same, and some substantial Vatican support in favor of this century's children, the status and future of the Catholic church and the efforts towards world peace would probably be far different than they appear to me today. My compliments and my respect.

You needn't bother answering this letter, really. I wrote it because I wanted to and hoped it would make a bright spot in your day. Besides, you're busy, and I'm incorrigible.

> Thank you again,
> Charles

Now he didn't have to write that. But you see it relates directly to what I've been saying: even though he came at Midnight Mass (or 10:30 Mass, or whenever it was), and even though the church was filled with imperfect people such as you and I are, he sensed something more than the sum total of our togetherness. He sensed spirit, prayer. Here's a cynic, an unbeliever, who has to confess that he was moved by the collective witness of the church, as imperfect as we are.

Though he said I needn't bother to answer his letter, I finally did, and I'd just like to read my reply and let it go at that:

Dear Charles:
As a sometimes infidel myself (faith's other side is doubt), I knew that, as you suggested, I needn't bother answering your letter. Then why do I find myself, exactly one month later, doing so? Many reasons, I guess.

First, I was moved by your charity to that lonely widow,

charity that led you both to a Catholic church, something your instincts would not normally allow.

Second, I was moved by your being moved by words, children, joy, and mostly, I would guess, the boldness of a gathered people who would dare rejoice even while aware of notices of betrayal in high places, both church and state; and a bomb ever over our collective heads.

Finally, I was moved by your very act of communicating your presence and your feelings. Slowly, I began to feel like Graham Greene's Monsignor Quixote, strangely drawn to his communist friend, Sancho.

And interestingly enough, there were, unknown to you, others like you in that gathering—and in our gatherings every weekend. Some of our choir are not Catholic. Some of our lectors have known the pain of divorce. Some are recovered cynics. Some are singles, like myself, who have found family. And some are just fellow journeyers who have come to the conclusion that if they do not know where the answer is, they know where it's not.

Not in technology alone, nor in the latest revolution, and certainly not in the salvations hawked by the media. Rather they sense that more of an answer, if there is one, will more likely be found in community, in caring, in celebrating; and for us that means gathering around the ancient wisdom of one who died for what he believed in.

Anyway, I'm taking the liberty, not knowing your tastes or journey, of sending you what I think might be an interesting book. You can return it read or unread.

Meanwhile, you're an interesting fellow pilgrim. You comfort and tantalize at the same time. Something's moving in your life. Follow it. You have my wishes, and more than that, my love and prayers.

                                        Father William Bausch

So here we are: the church of Jesus Christ. At times we are friendly, at times we are hostile. But still, we love each other. The church: our mother, our friend, and our enemy.

21

+

Caution and the Christ

Matthew 10:32–39

It happens in some friendships. It happens in some marriages. It happens in some schools. Friends or spouses for some reason have not learned complete trust. Their relationship is one of caution—always waiting for the other to make some betraying move. And if he or she does, then they are ready to declare that the friendship or the marriage is over.

Instead of total openness and communication, they have substituted judgment. Instead of taking the risk of completeness, they have substituted partiality. Instead of the poetry of surrender, they have substituted the prose of holding back—of waiting to see how things will turn out.

Such friendships and such marriages may last, and may last for a long while—until crisis time. Then the betrayal one *always* felt was there, the lack of trust one *always* knew was there, are enough to make one turn against one's friend, against one's spouse, and heap recriminations upon them and walk with them no more.

And, in many ways, this describes our tenuous relationship with Jesus, who is the Christ. Let me illustrate. There is a marvelous tale about love by the great master, Balzac, called *A*

Passion in the Desert. It tells of the rather strange relations between a stranded French soldier and a black panther in the
wilds and desert of Africa.

When the soldier and this panther first meet, they are wary
and cautious of each other and he, naturally, is half-frightened
to death. But gradually the man and the beast grow closer together. In fact, he calls the panther Monique, after an old love
of his.

They play together and hunt together and even look know-
ingly into one another's eyes. But for some reason, the soldier
always keeps his dagger at his side. On her part, at a certain
point in the story, the panther betrays a certain jealousy over
the soldier's interest in a handsome eagle that flies low over
them. She acts coquettishly, quivering as he strokes her head,
her eyes flashing like lightning just before she shuts them
tightly. And so it goes.

How do things come out between this mismatched pair in
the desert? Well, the two ended as all great passions end—by a
misunderstanding. You see, for some reason, in these passion-
ate relations one always suspects the other of infidelity and
treason. They each harbor thoughts about the other secretly,
and fail to come to an understanding through pride; and they
quarrel and part through sheer stubbornness. So one day the
soldier made a sudden move which was unimportant in itself
and to which he attached no significance. And Balzac tells the
story in his own words, as he has the soldier saying:

> I don't know if I hurt her, but she turned around as if en-
> raged, and with her sharp teeth she caught hold of my
> leg—gently, I daresay. But I, thinking she would devour
> me, plunged my dagger into her throat. She rolled over,
> giving a cry that froze my heart. And I saw her dying,
> looking at me without anger. I would have given all the
> world…to have brought her to life again.…
>
> The soldiers who had seen my flag, and were to come
> to my assistance, found me in tears.

We immediately think of our own lives and perhaps the

friendships we have wounded and the people we've hurt because we were too quick to interpret their motives, and sit in judgment of their actions. We really never trusted them; we were unwilling or unable to take the risk of surrendering all, so our communication, such as it was, was tainted with caution.

But what about the Christ in our lives?

Many people acquired a passion for him in youth. Many felt close to him when they were children. They felt his presence and knew his comfort and appreciated his love. And then—and then! He makes one false step—usually through his servants or the church—and we are ready to plunge the dagger into his throat.

There's the man who says that he's not going to Mass any more because he knows there are hypocrites there. So there are, and for them he will stab Christ and deny him.

He may argue that he's not denying Christ, but this will be true *only* if his discontinued community attendance truly and really makes him a better Christian. Only if he relates, through good works and prayer, more deeply to Christ. Only if Christ becomes more real to him. Otherwise, all along his relationship to Christ has been superficial and altogether too cautious. He failed to communicate his feelings, buckled under peer pressure. One false move from one of Christ's servants and he was quick with the dagger.

Or the girl who is a faithful Catholic until she acquires doubts about the church's teachings because they don't coincide with her feeling that "if you're in love it's all right to have sexual relations with your boyfriend," and it's only sensible to get the abortion because you're both still in school.

She interprets the "chastity before marriage and fidelity afterwards" as a false step, a mistake of the church and hardly the "in thing" in today's world.

So she draws her dagger, which takes the form of her feeling that she is losing her faith.

Or the man who doesn't believe in divorce until *his* marriage runs into difficulty and then, of course, "God will understand."

His relationship with Christ has not been totally trustworthy and so he is too facile in his judgments.

Or the woman who suddenly discovers sickness and suffering in her life and turns bitter against God. Her romance with God was fine up to that point, but now *God* is at fault and she quickly dispatches her belief.

Or the person who's met the bad Catholic, the scandalous priest, the insensitive brother or sister, and concludes that religion is basically a fraud, filled with fraudulent people.

Or the Catholic who feels that the church has betrayed him with all this renewal and change and turmoil. "It's not the same old church," which is like saying, "It's not the same old Christ"—which is like saying that he has no confidence in the Holy Spirit and in the church's proven ability to survive with the grace of God many, many renewals in its long history.

These are the Catholics who, for some reason, have kept their daggers at their sides. They have, perhaps, never made the leap of genuine faith in Christ Jesus. Oh, they played with him and hunted with him—but those daggers were always there. Deep down there was never a total trust and they may end the relationship by a misunderstanding.

They, for example, may want Jesus only when they need him, while *he* wants them all the time, and a misunderstanding arises. They may not understand that while they want to be comfortably holy, *he* wants them to be *uncomfortably* holy. They may not understand that while they want Jesus as a friend on the side along with other friends and things and goals, *he* is proclaiming that he, and only he, is the way and the truth and the life.

And you see what will happen. As we've just said: one sudden move, one false step on the part of Christ's servants or his church, one threatening move that Jesus might really pull their love into his all-embracing love—and in panic, the dagger is out and Christ lies dead, once more, rolled over, giving a cry that would freeze our hearts, and looking at us without anger.

Our caution killed him; that's what did it. Our lack of trust. Our inability to give total surrender. Our unwillingness to be open. Our rationalizations that made us think for the moment that he had betrayed us, while all the time we had betrayed him and ourselves, and thought we could sing the old song "We Shall Overcome" without him. And some day, those who see us may find us in tears.

22

+

Who Is Thomas's Twin?

John 20:19–31

If any of you have had twins, or know parents who have had twins, you can imagine what a double joy and a double challenge they must be. And even those of you who haven't had twins, after rejoicing—and wrestling—with a one- or two-year-old child all day long and finally nailing him or her into bed at night, you probably say, "Thank God there's not two of you. My energy only goes so far!"

I bring that up because the gospel seems to go out of the way to point out to us that Thomas was a twin. And I often wonder why they threw that detail in. Maybe his twin was one of the more well-known people in the early community, and that's why his being a twin is mentioned, but we don't know who this other twin was; and so speculation abounds.

We know it wasn't Peter and Andrew, or James and John, because they're listed as brothers and not triplets. Thomas could have been Matthew's twin, let's say; or maybe, more intriguingly, how about Mary Magdalene, his twin sister? Or perhaps it was Judas Iscariot, and that's why the twin's name isn't mentioned. But that's all speculation; we really don't know.

But none of this explains the real reason that the gospel writer made a point of mentioning that Thomas was a twin. There's another reason that's more profound. To the question "Who is Thomas's twin?"—the answer between the lines is evidently meant to be "us"! We are Thomas's twin, for all of us are a mixture of fear and doubt, pessimism and trust, belief and unbelief. And that's a difficult place to be, because for every one of us, our human condition has such a hankering for certainty.

We see this even in the sciences. Every few years they revise the latest science, the latest theory. Recently the U.S. launched a special telescope up into the atmosphere. There's just a yearning and a longing and a desire to know; and not only to know, but to know for certain. But as urgent as the desire to know is in everybody, I think it trebles when we deal with life and human relationships. For us it would be expressed this way:

"If only I had the certainty of some sign."

"What kind of certainty?"

"Well, a sign, for example, that there is a God. I'm not sure there is. I'm not positive there isn't. I don't know it. I say I believe it, but wouldn't it be nice to have an unmistakable sign that there is a God? Wouldn't it be nice to know for certain that it's going to be all right in the end? With all of the nonsense and the hardships and difficulty of life, wouldn't it be good to know that it's going to be all right? All the evil people will get their comeuppance, all the good people will be rewarded; virtue will be vindicated."

I think a lot of us could put up with much more if we only knew at the end it's going to be all right. If only, in all the absurdities of life—babies are born with AIDS, people get cancer, and people are starving as I speak to you, and the inhumanity of man to man, as the saying goes—if only we at least knew that at the end God would have the final vindicating word, we could then put up with that kind of absurdity.

We would like to be certain that our spouse, without a shadow of a doubt, really loves us, that we really count to somebody in this world, that no matter what happens, there's some-body who loves us with a deep and unalloyed and uncondi-tional love. We want to be the apple, the sun, the moon, of somebody's eye. If we had that as a certainty, we could put up with an awful lot, couldn't we?"

But the fact is we don't have that certainty, and so we be-come Thomas's twin. And what does the scripture say about that condition? Well, as usual, the Scripture doesn't give us a direct answer; it leaves room for faith. But we get in this gospel at least some hints and approaches, some commentary about dealing with uncertainty.

And one of the more obvious commentaries in the gospel—again, you can read between the lines—is that Thomas was ab-sent. Now there could have been many reasons why he was absent. After all, his band had just broken up, his leader was captured and horribly crucified. Everything that he believed in, everything that he had given himself to, has just collapsed. I'm sure he must have been depressed. I would presume he wanted to be alone, like many of us in tragedy and hardship; he just was withdrawn. But even though the gospel sympa-thizes with that, it at once makes a sharp commentary. The fact is, he missed out. The fact is, not being part of the church of fellowship, Thomas missed out. And that's always a mistake.

It's a mistake of people who say, "I don't have to go to church. I can worship God in my own way." And I remember a wise old priest, when someone once told him that, and it was a winter's day and he had the fire going, all he did was to get up and take out a glowing piece of coal and put it on the stone hearth. As both of them watched, in a very short time the coal went out. For the coal to maintain itself it needed the fellow-ship of the other coals.

And this was Thomas's mistake. Even though he was de-pressed and withdrawn and shattered, he should not have left the fellowship because he could never find his way by himself, that's for sure. He had to have some kind of faith, and faith is gained and shared and matured in fellowship. Faith is doubt positioned in hope. And where does hope come from? It comes from other people. All of us have our doubts, but to cope with them, we need each other.

Some people seem to have a mistaken notion that if you believe in a church, let us say if you become a Catholic, you surrender your critical faculties. You hand over your mind to Pope John Paul. He's got the key to your mind and intelligence. And doubt, therefore, is not permitted. But the truth is the contrary, because for many people doubt is often a sign of spiritual earnestness. You have to believe that. Doubt is a sign of spiritual earnestness—at least you're struggling. The Bible is filled with famous doubters, from Job to Jonah. And all of us have cause to doubt.

And when does doubt become most severe? Obviously in tragic times, particularly if people are in a kind of childish mode with God. That is, "Look, I go to church every Sunday, I keep the commandments, I say my prayers. How could you let my daughter die? How could you let my spouse walk out on me? How could you let me get sick?"

And that's where the doubt really comes in. "After I've done everything for you, God, you turn around and do this to me."

And even though that's a kind of childish relationship to God, doubt is strong.

But what the Scripture is saying is that having such doubts is understandable because, like Thomas, in everybody's life we experience the absent Christ. There's nothing wrong with that, and nothing to be ashamed of. It's a reality of all relationships. There's hardly a husband or wife who has not doubted the other at one time. There's hardly the most fervent friendship that hasn't had its weak moments. And there's hardly a believer who hasn't known Christ absent from his or her life.

But the scripture again is strong and challenging because it says that we, like Thomas, must remain in or return to our faith community and there we too must cry out, "My Lord and my God!" even when that's more of a question than it is a statement.

Every Christian is at a different place in life's journey on this pilgrimage of ours. There are some up front who have never flinched and have always carried the banner "Jesus Christ Is Lord," and they've never wavered from the time they were born until the time they die. Well, good for them. Then there's the other extreme, in the back, trailing up the hind quarters, not sure that they should even be in this parade to begin with. And I guess the vast majority of us are in the middle: we waver between moving up front and lagging behind.

But no matter where we are in our pilgrimage—and it's perfectly all right to be of strong faith or weak faith—the important thing is simply to be on the pilgrimage at all. That is a sign of vitality. That's a sign of that earnestness of which I spoke. It is a sign I haven't, like Thomas, just absented myself and withdrawn, because then I really will go wrong. I'm not my own measurement. I need the witness and I need the discernment of others. I could not survive in my faith, in my religion, or this Catholic church without you. I hope you cannot survive without one another, wherever we are in the parade.

So this is a gospel about us, and I think that is precisely why the question was raised. In a little parenthesis it says: "Thomas was a twin." And it leaves us with that tantalizing question: Who is that twin? Well, to paraphrase Pogo: "We must have met him, and he is us."

23

✛

Not One Stone Upon Another
Luke 21:1–28

This kind of gospel is called apocalyptic, apocalyptic in the sense that it points to terrible, terrible things that are going to happen. The gospel does not so much reflect the words of Jesus, as it reflects the writer's outlook, because in fact Luke was writing this gospel in what we would call apocalyptic times.

Jerusalem had been barbarously invaded by the Romans and razed to the ground. The Temple had been torn down. To appreciate that, think, as Roman Catholics, of St. Peter's in Rome being bombed to smithereens. That's what it was for them, and even more. Bodies lying all over the streets, mass deportations. At the time of this gospel, the people were standing in the midst of ruin.

Again, if you want to appreciate the mentality behind the gospels, just imagine that you live on one of the Caribbean islands that was devastated a while back by Hurricane Hugo and you're standing in rubble, pulling out bodies from under the debris, wondering where and how you will ever rebuild. Or think of the catastrophic earthquake in San Francisco. Or think of the terrible storms we had recently, and think of those school children suddenly being killed when a tornado hit their school, and the wreck of the school. But more importantly, the wreck of the lives of innocent children, and their parents, who have to cope with that. Think of Beirut, Lebanon, called the Garden City of the East, now reduced to a pile of ruins.

Well, this is the vantage point of Luke, who wrote this gospel. His world was collapsing and all was devastation, as happens in different parts of history. This sort of thing happened again a little more than five hundred years after Luke wrote this gospel, around the year 600. We have a record from Pope Gregory the Great, Pope Gregory I.

At that time the Saracens were pirating the seas. The barbarians had overrun Rome and the whole peninsula. The government had collapsed; there was no government; it fled. The Roman senate and the Roman emperor took off for Constantinople. Gregory wrote these words: "What Rome herself, once mistress of the world, has become, we now see. Wasted away with afflictions, the loss of citizens, the assault of enemies, the frequent fall of ruined buildings. Where is the senate? Where are the people? All gone. All the pomp and dignity of this world is gone."

And he, too, stood among the rubble of a Rome that was in ruins. And yet, as St. Luke's followers, what did he and the other Christians do? Gregory and his other clergy simply took the rubble and they rebuilt. Gregory started food lines. And if it weren't for Gregory, whole masses of civilizations would have starved. They opened up monasteries, the hospitality inns of the day. They kept alive the flame of learning. The whole social system had broken down. They took over the government because there was a vacuum. There was nobody there to do it. And Gregory never saw, and never knew, that in fact he was laying the foundation of Western civilization; he didn't know that any more than Luke could have realized that two thousand years after he wrote his words of devastation you and I would listen to the same word and break the same bread because of Luke and Gregory.

In any case, significantly, Pope Gregory rejected the title of Universal Patriarch, and instead he took the title that the popes still use: The Servant of the Servants of the Lord. But Gregory himself never saw the fruit of his work. He never realized that he was preparing for a future and not living at the end of the times.

You say, "Well, what does this gospel have to do with us?" This much: Our times are very much like those last days about which the gospel is written. Luke describes it as Jesus saying that there will not be one stone left upon another, and all of us have witnessed the stones of our civilization falling one by one. The papers talk about Los Angeles gangs and tell us that they have to have counter-gangs stand at the school doors so that various people can go to school safely. Schools in different parts of the United States—in New York and New Jersey, for instance—have guards in the corridor. A student went to school and was shot to death the other day. There is crime in the streets. Stability has crumbled. Families have crumbled. The divorce rates, the broken homes, the infidelity. Common decency has crumbled. Drugs are the cancer of our society. The crimes, the wasted lives. Innocent children born addicted. The "boarder babies" waiting for someone to pick them up and hug them. The future psychopaths fifteen years from now. The babies born with AIDS. The six Jesuits killed in their college in San Salvador. Stones are tumbling down. Not one stone is left upon another.

And yet on the other hand there is another kind of stone that has come down, and that's the stone of repression. Think of the Berlin Wall. Who would have thought years ago that that wall would come tumbling down? That communism would decay so quickly? That people's thirst and sacrifice for freedom would pay off so quickly? And you and I, from a distance, watched these people literally climbing over and through a wall that has symbolically, and actually, broken down.

And that is a part of what this gospel is about because as this gospel talks about the apocalyptic time of St. Luke, it also tells us about the times when decent people rebuilt. And the fact is that we, like Gregory, can lay the foundation of a Christian culture once more. There are usually three steps to this, three statements that we can make about the rebuilding that you and I are entrusted with, even though we don't see the fruits of it.

The first is: begin with what you have. Look at what you have. Never mind what's crumbled, never mind what's diseased, never mind what's wrong. Look at what you have.

A man told me a while back about an experience he had in Dublin. He woke up very angry because the people at the desk were supposed to wake him up half an hour earlier and they never did. "To add insult to injury," he said, "I was further irritated when the service delivered bacon and eggs, and I had ordered boiled eggs. And they gave me *The Irish Times* instead of *The Daily Telegraph* that I ordered. So I picked up the phone and I complained to the desk, and the girl, in her typical lovely Irish way, responded, 'Well, now,' she said, 'you're awake, aren't you? You've got something to eat and something to read while you eat. I say you're not badly off.'"

Look at what you have, not at what you lost, or wish was there. The first step in rebuilding is to look to God. Look what by the grace of God you have.

The second step the gospel would tell is: look at what is possible. Some of you know the name Glenn Cunningham. When he was seven years old, his legs were so badly damaged that the doctors considered amputation. And at the last minute they decided against it. And one of the doctors patted Glenn's shoulder and said, "When the weather gets warm we'll get you in a chair and you can sit on the porch."

And Glenn said, "No, I don't want to sit on the porch. I want to walk and I want to run, and I will." And the doctor just shook his head and walked away. Well, two years later Glenn was running; he wasn't running fast, but he was running. And eventually Glenn went to college, and his extracurricular activity was track. He was running not only to prove the doctors wrong, but because he soon became good at it. And soon the intercollegiate records began to fall beneath his driving legs. Then came the Berlin Olympics. Glenn not only qualified for the Berlin Olympics, but he broke the Olympic record for the fifteen-hundred meter race. The following year Glenn broke the indoor mile record. The boy who wasn't supposed to walk again became the fastest man on earth. Look what is possible.

And the third step the gospel would tell us is: look what can be done. In 1930 a traveler was exploring the French Alps, and he came upon a vast stretch of barren land. It was completely empty, it was ugly, it was utterly desolate. It was the kind of place that you keep away from. And then suddenly the traveler stopped in his tracks. In the middle of this vast wasteland was a bent-over old man; he was walking along with a four-foot iron pipe; every few feet he was stamping the pipe in the ground; and he was dropping acorns into the holes. The traveler got to speak with him, and the man told him: "I planted over a hundred thousand acorns. Perhaps only a tenth of them will survive."

And then the traveler learned that the old man's wife had died and his son had died in a tragic accident. And the old man decided not what was, but he decided what could be done. And he said that he wanted to spend his last days doing something creative and something good. He said, "I want to do something useful."

Well, thirty-five years later this traveler went back—now older and wiser himself—to this same stretch of land, and he could hardly believe his eyes. What he saw just amazed him. The land was covered with a beautiful forest. Birds were in the trees, wild animals were living there. It was a magnificent sight. And all because someone cared. Look at what can be done.

So basically, what the gospel is telling us as we listen to these terrible, apocalyptic, dire, horrible things happening, is that we can rebuild through a life of faith, you and I. That's been entrusted to us. The only thing that I can tell you is what you already know: there's no rebuilding by yourself. It's a moral, physical, mental, and psychological impossibility. We need one another. We need a faith community to reaffirm our values and encourage our hearts. We need our common sacramental life to celebrate the special moments in our common journey. We need our parish to gather us around the altar and the works of justice and mercy that flow from it. We need our long list of saints who have been through it all, those witnesses who help us remember what we have, what is possible, and what can be done.

We *do* have a heritage and a tradition on which to build in these apocalyptic times and to pass on to our children. And we have a long line of people like Luke and Gregory to encourage us to pray more sincerely the words of today's canon, "Help us to work together for the coming of your Kingdom."

24

✝

The Great Commandment and the Retarded

Matthew 22:34–40

In the Mosaic Law, the Hebrews had counted up 613 commandments. And so there was always speculation as to which of these 613 was the greatest; and the discussion of that was a typical rabbinical enterprise.

And so they brought Jesus this common question, and Jesus answers them with the traditional Hebrew shema. That is, he joins a quotation from Deuteronomy about loving God with your whole heart and soul, to a quotation from Leviticus saying to love your neighbor as yourself. This is not the first time that the two of them were joined. We find such a joining in the Testaments of the Twelve Patriarchs. But they are here in the gospel, side by side, as a kind of summary.

What is new from Jesus is that these two commandments are intertwined; they are interlocked. They are so interrelated that one is not valid without the other. So the heritage we have from the gospel is that the love of God and the love of neighbor are inseparable. Hence it becomes necessary for us to look at that neighborly love and, ultimately, at the question of social justice. It becomes necessary for us to look at our responsibilities, not only to our next-door neighbor, but to our global neighbors as well.

And that forces us to consider that we, as the population of the United States, are only 6 percent of the world's population, and yet, through the encouragement of commercial advertising, we consume 33 percent of the world's resources and energy. And we are forced to realize that this can't go on; and that the rest of the world, of course, is quite angry with us and they are determined to have a fair share of the world's resources; and if they will not get the share by persuasion, they indeed will take it by revolutionary violence.

Therefore, this question of love of God and neighbor is critically important, perhaps for our survival. But, as important as the global implications are, I would here like to narrow down my comments to a seldom thought of aspect of the love of neighbor and God. The aspect I speak of is the retarded neighbor, child or adult. I know something of this from personal experience because my nephew is retarded. He has a type of Mongolism. I remember being in the hospital room when my brother-in-law broke the news to my sister. She was quiet for a very long time and then she said to her husband, "We asked for a child; we didn't ask for a perfect child." And that was that.

And being somewhat interested and learning something about this, I have discovered that parents usually have one or more of five reactions to a brain-damaged or retarded or defective child or to a child who has simply become a tremendous problem.

The first reaction which seems to be so common and universal—whether the child is retarded or whether you have an older son or daughter who has hurt you and gone off and is living with somebody, or something like that—is guilt. Guilt always seems to be the nearest emotion. "What did I do wrong? How did my children turn out to be like that? Maybe if I had done something better in bringing him or her up...."

Or it's the guilt—"Well, is there something basically wrong in my chromosomes and genes? There must be something wrong if *we* produced a defective child." But of course there's no truth to that whatsoever, and a child who is brain-damaged or defective or hurt can, as a matter of fact, appear and happen at any particular time.

The second reaction is for parents simply to refuse to acknowledge what has happened. It's clear to all and to the doctor there's something wrong with this child, but they look away and say it's nothing, the child will outgrow it; and just pretend that the "something" is not there.

The third reaction is, thank heaven, very rare: it is responding with total rejection. I know one couple who, immediately after the child was born and proved to be defective, put him in an institution, which of course is fine to that extent; but they have never seen or visited the child and have never acknowledged that the child is alive, to this day, some thirty years later. They've just out and out rejected the child.

Perhaps the most common reaction, understandably, is over-protection, focusing too much attention on the child because the child is defective in some way. The parents make the whole family or whole community center around that child which often, of course, is not the best for the child because a child at any stage can learn some self-reliance and often over-protecting parents pre-empt that. I remember once talking to a group of parents of retarded children, and I was talking about this. After the talk was over one thirteen-year-old boy came up (and he was retarded) and he said, "I'm glad you said that and that my parents were here to listen," because he had wanted to go away to a camp for retarded children and his mother wouldn't let him. His mother thought he might get hurt, he might get homesick, and so forth and so on. As a result of listening, she finally agreed to let him go. You shouldn't over-protect them. They should be given the chance to do what they can do.

The final reaction is the most mature of all, whether the child is perfectly normal or retarded, and refers to adults as well. This reaction is to accept these human beings as they are, not imposing what they cannot be or should not be. I know a family, the O'Donnells, who have nine children. One of their children, Michael, was born defective. He was blind, mentally retarded, unable to walk, and unable to speak. The doctors said that he would be a vegetable all his life. After the initial shock, Jack and Kitty just decided that they were not going to believe this and they were not going to over-protect Michael.

And with eight other brothers and sisters jollying him along and fighting and squabbling and all that, treating him as normally as they could, chastising him when he was bad and naughty, spanking him when he didn't do things right, that child came along beyond all expectations. He learned to walk. He could hear. He learned to speak, however haltingly. And even though he was blind, Michael could pick out voices. I used to go to the ballfield to watch the kids play and I would come up and say, "Hi, Mike," and he would say, "Hi, Father Bausch."

So because of the love of his family, because they refused to cater to him, because they refused to allow him to just be a vegetable all of his life, this kid developed way beyond anybody's expectations.

Some of you may know the name Dale Francis. He's a columnist for *Our Sunday Visitor*. He has some lovely things to say that I'd like to share with you. He has a retarded son named Guy, and here's what he writes:

I wish Guy were normal, of course, but he isn't. He is my son and I love him; love him not as the young man he might have been, but as the son who is. That's the secret. Only it really isn't a secret. If we are given children, we must love them as they are. And there are many satisfactions, in a sense, perhaps, more special satisfactions than we have from our normal children because even small achievements have an importance.

So my son, Guy, I love him. Sometimes when I see signs of the leadership he might have shown, the compassion he possesses, I have a twinge of sadness for the man he might have been, but it doesn't stay with me even a second. I love him for who he is.

I said there are small achievements that can give you great satisfaction. I remember one of them. One day I was busy writing and typing when Guy wanted my attention. I kept up with my work. He came up to me and showed me pictures he had drawn, and I said they were nice, and I went on working. He wrote "Guy"—the only word he knows how to write—and I said that was good and went on working.

He was away for a little while and then he came to me, smiling big. "Look, Daddy," he said, and handed me another piece of paper. There he had written in big, but crooked letters, "DALE," my name. How he had written it I do not know. He had never done it before; he has never done it since. But he did it that day. He held it up to me proudly. "That's very good, Guy," I said. "Do you want me to play with you now?"

He grinned, and I left my typewriter. And so we sat down and drew airplanes and cows and trains, and I thought there must not be many fathers who would gain a sense of joy in seeing a twenty-year-old son's writing of a name.

So what does all this have to do with the gospel before us? It has to do with the gospel because it is an object lesson. For instance, at Halloween you see children in their costumes and your very first reaction might be to the costume and the mask. But underneath the mask and the costume is a child of God and a potential saint; and ultimately, a spark of the divine—of God. We learn to love through the mask to the person, and once we learn to love through the mask, we learn to love God; and that's what the gospel is saying.

The point is that to truly love our neighbors we must learn to look and love beyond what first catches our eye. Some kids may have slow minds, poor motor control, crooked mouths and crazy laughs. But above all, they are italicized examples and forceful reminders to love through those characteristics and really see the person who is there. When we take delight in a twenty-year-old person spelling out four letters in the alphabet, when in those moments we see and know that a real and beautiful person is there, when we love that person—then we are fulfilling the law of God and really loving God.

The retarded child and the retarded adult, whether they have very minor or very major defects, are our surprises and challenges. They are living invitations that the love of neighbor and the love of God can never, never be separated.

25

Entering Passiontide

John 11:1–45

Passiontide lies before us, and our scriptural theme—as revealed in the powerful gospel story of Lazarus—is death and life and the power of Christ. We are about to celebrate, if that's the right word, the confrontation of death with life itself—Jesus on the cross.

In order to enhance what the liturgy wants us to resonate with, I'd like to restate our scriptural theme in terms of an old Russian legend entitled "How Death Became Life." The legend helps to give focus to these last days of Lent. The story goes like this:

Death was born on a flaming day; at least that was the way she remembered it. And when she came forth full grown into this world, it was alight with all the colors afire. The light seemed to come from a sword which an immense angel held aloft guarding a door to she knew not where.

At first, death felt like a stranger. She wandered kind of lost, then one day she saw a beautiful bird with gorgeous white plumage. Gently she walked up to it and stretched out her hand to feel the softness of the feathers which shone like the sun on the bird's back. But no sooner had her fingers touched it than the bird fell at her feet, cold and still. Death picked it up and wondered why it had stopped singing and stopped living. And that was how she discovered her dreaded power. And that is how she understood why she had been born on a flaming day.

Well, slowly the years flowed into eternity where all time goes, and death traveled through them all touching now this animal and that bird, and this fish or that flower. By then she knew the earth very well, and she had noticed that a certain kind of creature, human beings, dwelt in it, who still held in their faces a strange reflection of God. It was as though they had been made in the image of God.

Well, death took a long time to touch humankind, but one day she did, and she saw them shudder. They cried out and became as cold and still as that first bird with the white plumage that she touched. And on that day death tasted the fullness of her awesome power, but on that day, also, she knew loneliness to the very last drop.

Well from then on, as the centuries turned into thousands of years and thousands of years into millions, death claimed all living things for her own. Yet there was in her a hunger that grew. In her silent kingdom nothing remained. All living things crumbled and turned into dust at her touch. She was always left with loneliness. There were days, years even, when death almost went mad with loneliness, with the desire to have and to hold something that would last, someone or something that she could call her own.

Well, it was now a great time of plagues and storms and floods, and with tears flowing down her emaciated cheeks, death crisscrossed the whole earth with the swiftness born of frenzied hunger. Throwing herself at the children of human beings, she embraced them passionately, hoping against hope that she might see a smile or hear a word that would lift the pall of her loneliness that isolated her from all living things and held her tighter and tighter.

But she learned that human beings feared her above all things. They shrank from her approach. They invented thousands of legends about her trying to pretend that she was really incapable of harming them. They even began to imagine a life after death that was somehow a continuation of the earthly life that they knew here. Slowly the legends that they made up grew into religious beliefs and centered on ways and means of escaping death. Their attempts left a wide trail of artifacts scattered over the earth, and other humans would dig in the bowels of the earth to trace this trail.

But death kept walking the earth. At times she smiled at human beings' subtle fear of her, and she enjoyed her power over them. At other times she wept bitterly, not only because she was lonely, but because she sensed that there was always some part of each human being that seemed to escape her. One day, the story goes, tired and weary, she sat on a hill beneath three crosses on which three men were being executed. She did not feel like looking at or touching any one of these. She was too tired, and she was too lonely, and she was too disconsolate. So she just sat there, her weary head in her hands, and she wept slow, huge tears, bemoaning her loneliness.

Suddenly above her she heard a voice say, "I thirst." She looked up. Her gaze met two fathomless eyes. From their depths flowed a brilliant, warm, blue light, the likes of which she had never experienced before. Instantly she stood up, rigid, erect, tall, and thin. A few paces away this man hung between two others. She somehow did not dare to look at him though she wanted, more than she had ever wanted, to touch him, and to touch him with love and respect. Yet very self-consciously she put her hands behind her back and stared at this bleeding, disfigured face, as if she could never see enough.

She heard him speak some short sentences. Each word she locked into her heart. She relished them. The very echo of the voice weak with pain and hunger moved her deeply. Then he was silent, but his eyes called to her in a wordless message. She did not know how it happened, but gently, ever so gently, she touched his cheek. He seemed for an instant to smile for her alone. Then like all the others before him, he closed his eyes and became lifeless and cold.

She could not believe it. Somehow she knew without knowing that he was different from all the others. So she lingered awhile. She saw him taken down from the cross. She saw his mother hold his lifeless body in her arms and cradle the ashen face against her bosom. She saw him being carried into a grave in the hollow of a cave. She saw some soldiers roll the stone to the entrance of the cave in order to seal it. Then, fleet on foot and noiseless as only death can be, she entered the cave just before the stone was put in place.

What passed between him and death no human being will ever know. But one thing is certain. On the following Sunday, two days after he had been taken down from his cross, some women came to the tomb and it was empty. Death was not there. And since that Sunday morning, all who look upon death with the eyes of faith see it differently. They know that love is life, and death is now but the gate to eternal life.

That's an old Russian legend that talks about the same thing the scriptures talk about. As a poet put it:

Is there a leaf upon the tree
The Father does not see?
Leaves fall, so do we all
Return to earth, to sod.
Sparrows and kings
And all manner of things
Fall, fall, into the hands
Of the living God.

As we walk with Jesus these final days before Easter, let us try to understand that the only possible force that could overcome death was God's love in Christ. And that includes not only our physical death, it includes the death of the soul, which we call sin. And anyone who is burdened with guilt and sin and a sense of deadliness, anyone burdened with the pain of death—the death of a relationship—that's sad. The death of a marriage—that's sad. The death of a friendship; the death of children's love for you; the death of all kinds of things, however it's spelled out—all these are causes of great sadness. And the scripture tells us, and the story retells us, that the only thing that overcomes death is God's love in Jesus.

So in these few days that remain before Holy Week, perhaps there are several ways we can go to meet this love. All of the deadly things in our lives, including sin, we hand over to Christ, perhaps in a good Easter confession. "Bless me, Father, I have sinned. I have known death. I want to be alive again. Bless me, Father, I am burdened, I want the burden lifted. Bless me, Father, I know evil. I want to know goodness."

So again Christ waits high on his cross, to take away that death. And for those who know other kinds of death—physical or moral or mental—again, in these last weeks, go to Christ in prayer, go and turn over your life to him, and say, "Here I am. Only you have this power. Only your love is stronger than the strongest thing on earth."

And so death herself found out that in Jesus she was powerless. And death's loneliness found fulfillment in Christ; and the message is that so can ours.

So these are important days. Passiontide's coming, the great Holy Week. Be prepared now in your prayerfulness, in your life, and in your love, to turn over that life and love to Christ. And in that turning over be prepared to discover newness, fulfillment, and the words of a friend who weeps over us, calling us by name: Mary (or John)—"come forth."

And though we have been bound, like Lazarus, with constriction and sin and fault and problems, life returns, death is defeated, and love once more has triumphed.

26

✝

The Meaning of Advent

Mark 13:33–37

The church has its own calendar, and in the church's calendar the new year begins with the first Sunday of Advent. If Advent is to mean anything in reference to a new year, we have to explore what it means in reference to Christmas, because it is closely related to Christmas; to see precisely where we got the feast, we have to begin with Christmas, which is a late feast, beginning around the fourth century. It wasn't celebrated around the Christian world for almost four hundred years.

In order better to understand Christmas and Advent, we have to go back to pagan times when the celebrations started. The pagans saw the world as a great cosmic struggle between the powers of darkness and the powers of light. And they noticed as they watched that at different times darkness seemed to be getting more of the light, so to speak. They were watching, if you will, two great cosmic wrestlers and every once in a while they would see that the wrestler called darkness would pin down the light and be ready to do it in. They noticed this because the days at this time of the year were getting shorter. If they were getting shorter that meant that the light, or the sun, was getting weaker. And as darkness pinned the sun to its back, and was ready to dispatch it, they noticed the sun getting weaker and those dark days getting longer and longer. And they were afraid that someday darkness would kill the sun and the light, until around December 21.

Around December 21 they noticed that the tables began to turn, and that the sun was regaining its strength (just like wounded heroes in those old cowboy movies we see), and suddenly the hero who was pinned down against the rock or on the ground, with an adversary over him, ready to stab him, gets a burst of strength and flips him over and climbs on top of him and starts pinning him down.

Well, they noticed that. The sun suddenly got a second wind and all of a sudden was beginning to push darkness off and against the wall. They understood this because around December 21 the days started getting longer. It means that darkness was getting weak and the sun was getting strong. And so when this happened, the pagans celebrated the resurrection, or the coming, or the light of the sun. It was a sun feast, marking the transition time from darkness to light.

When the Christians came along they took over this pagan notion. They said, "It's a pretty good notion that you've got here, and after all, we know that if you're really talking about darkness and light, the only real darknesses of this world are the darkness of sin and the darkness of death. And the only light in this world is Jesus. So we'll keep the notions."

But what the Christians did, as it were, they took the word "sun" and they took out the middle letter, "u," and they changed it to "o." So the sun they were talking about was Jesus, the Son of God, and they made this time of year a celebration when we would get ready for the tables to be turned. In the great struggle, this was the time when sin and death would now be overcome by the light of the world, Jesus, the S-o-n of God. So they called this time Christmas, and they made Advent the time of considering an end of darkness and looking forward to the coming light.

And that's what it has meant to us Christians ever since.

Christmas is the beginning. The passion, death, and resurrection are the final burst, and the victory of the Son of God. But Christmas is the beginning, and Advent marks that time when darkness grows weaker and the sun becomes stronger. And so Advent became, and still remains for us, a time when the tide will turn. If you see it that way, you get a good understanding.

Advent is supposed to be a time of breakthrough—from darkness into light. It is truly our new year, and that's why you notice that the scripture is speaking about the end. Jesus says, "Be on guard, it will come like a thief in the night." And the next gospel will talk about the sun falling and the moon not giving its light. What Jesus is talking about is not the end of our material world; what Jesus and the scriptures mean is, "Okay, this is an end to darkness. Get ready to move into light."

Advent, then, is a challenge. Advent simply comes to us very forcefully with a question: What is the struggle in your life and mine? Advent asks: What do you want to overcome? Advent asks: What darkness in your life and your world would you like to see reversed?

What breakthrough would you and I want for this new year? What tide would you like turned around? That you might be more understanding? More kind? More forgiving? Less addicted? More chaste? Holier? Closer to God? Better personality? That people would like you? That your job or your marriage would flourish? That your children or parents would change? That school would be more attractive? What dark things in your life would you like to see reversed? If you had to pick a theme or a motif for this coming year, what would you pick? Let me made a suggestion.

Bear with me as I read from a lovely book by George Leach. Just listen and see what catches you, and we'll relate it to Advent.

What is happening in family life these days? If we believed everything that appears in the public press, the future looks dismal. Divorce and separation pour down like a monsoon. Infidelity is like an ever-flooding river. Many people ponder whether marriage is possible. The young flounder when they see the floods of non-commitment. Inter-family strife sends adolescents running. Where? To dope, to booze, to sex. The pain is excruciating in so many. Is there any hope?

Single people often seem to be stalking the streets in isolation. The lonely crowd, the gang of isolated individuals, even couples on a date who talk *at* and not *with* each other—all reveal the wrenching pain of loneliness.

The apartment dwellers cut themselves off at the fifteenth story behind locked doors. The aged peer from behind wise eyes, having no one with whom to share. The alcoholic, drunk again, stumbles in his latest stupor. The prostitute, male or female, sells his or her body. Where is the relationship? Is love possible? What do we fear? What are we running from?

Or we can take a look at the people in our institutions. Our hospitals are becoming more crowded and less staffed. What does this say of patient care? The stress among nurses, doctors, and support staff grows. How do they handle financial cutbacks and rotating shift work, to mention only two problems? How will we meet the tensions of our penal institutions? Or the mental patient escapes? The papers panic. Fear floods the heart of man, but what will he do?

What does one say to the unwanted child? To a single parent? To a divorcee? What can we do for them, or might we dare suggest? How can we live with the labeled person? He's handicapped, retarded, strange they say; but what do we say?

What crosses our minds when we read about the labor disputes? High school teachers on strike? The uprising that caused the university explosions a few years back?

So much personal suffering and hidden pain exists around us, indeed in many of us. If we dare to look into the mirror, pause and reflect, we might break the mirror and run. Does irritation ever lead us to frustration? Even anger and hostility? A simple comment can shift our mood. A glance can change our feelings. Maybe fear lurks in the recesses of our being. What will trigger the emotional reaction that scares us, frightens us, unleashes fear? Maybe domination and control pervade our lives. We need to have everything just so. Or more subtly, we control others by our compliments. Manipulation is another manifestation. However we cut it, pride is rampant.

Healing is necessary. Maybe one of the deepest and most crippling pains is self-pity. The "poor me" attitude squeaks out of so many. People feel so sorry for themselves that they can be emotional paralytics. Lost in their own world, they spiral into isolation and become grossly unattractive to others. They despair as they are tossed on their sea of hopelessness. Their very problems compound their problem. Our world needs so much healing. Our country needs so much healing. We need so much healing. And it begins with us. Where, then? And how—will we begin?

My dear friends, I might suggest that in our new year we begin today. If you and I are looking for a motif, and we want to roll back some of that darkness, I might suggest the motif of healing. You and I realize the incredible fact that we contain within us—within our very look, within our very hand, our very lips—the power to heal. A gesture to make somebody feel better. A smile. Picking up the telephone. A courteous note. An apology given. A love spoken. A reach outward. A very simple thing; and yet we can heal hearts and souls—and often bodies. We have that power. That should be our goal for the new year.

We live in darkness. Others live in darkness. We can roll it back. We can help the sun to rise. We can make the day brighter for everyone—just by a glance, by a word, by a look, by an unspoken love. And yet—we cannot do this without Jesus. If anything profound is going to happen to us this year, it will have to be in relationship with Jesus Christ.

We've got to get to know him better. He's not just a name, he's what draws us to the church. He's got to be a reality in our lives. He's got to be a friend. He's got to be personal. He's got to be deep. He's got to be someone that we speak of. He's got to be someone that we speak to, someone that we speak from. We've got to look at the world through his eyes, and touch with his hands, and hear with his ears.

If darkness is to be rolled back, it's you and I who will do it. If you're looking for something for Advent, Advent is a time when there's a turnabout, the breakthrough. What breakthrough would you like? If we're to be free from sin, and from your problems and my problems, and your sins and my sins, we need each other.

That's one of the great rationales for the little Advent box, and I hope you take advantage of it—to put in your name and take out the name of a stranger, and pray for one another. It's not a gimmick, it is gospel. We've gotta lift each other's darkness. We've gotta turn the tide. Advent is that kind of season. It's that patient struggle. That patient living in the light which is Jesus so that the positions can be reversed. And darkness, which has you and me pinned to the wall, we can, in turn, overcome.

In the early part of the gospel, when Jesus is just starting his public ministry, he asks one of the apostles, I think Nathaniel, to follow him. Nathaniel says, "Where do you live?" And Jesus simply says, "Come and see." How about that?

Jesus, where do you live? He lives in somebody's darkness. Come and see. Somebody's hurting, somebody's in pain, somebody's in grief, somebody's struggling. Even those who seem the most cheerful and they've got it all together—it doesn't impress me at all—I've seen altogether too many of those people fall apart. And all that they ever wanted, all that you and I ever wanted, was to be healed with the affirming touch of another.

If this world, if this nation, if you and I as a community are to roll back the darkness, Advent's the time. A new year, a new beginning, a time when darkness begins to slip. And hopefully in your life and mine, the Son, Jesus, begins to rise.

27

✝

Lost and Found

1 Timothy 1:12–17

We know the story of the prodigal son so well that it might be worth our time to look at the theme, not so much from the gospel, but through the eyes of St. Paul. And if you attended to this epistle and to this little bit of revelation of Paul's life, there are two points that come across quite strongly.

The first point is Paul's open proclamation that like the prodigal son, he had experienced the sense and the pain of being lost. This sense of being lost is not uncommon. As people progress through different stages of life they sense this pain.

Oh, there are many ways of becoming lost. For example, some just drift away. You know, it's one of those things. You say to your husband or wife, "You know, looking back I guess it's been four or five years since we've seen Harry and Jane." It's not that you broke off, not that there's been any big argument; it's just that you've drifted apart. People drift apart from friendships, people drift away from faith. And all of a sudden they are alert one day—nothing big and traumatic—to a sense of loss.

As the farmer said when he was bringing home his stray calf and the city man asked him how they get lost: "They just nibble themselves lost." And it's true. They just nibble, heads down, toward the green grass and go from one green patch to another, right through a hole in the fence, and lo and behold, they can't get back. Some people suddenly sense loss like that.

Others have a sense of loss through world problems. None of us faces the world problems directly because they're too oppressive, but out of the corner of our eye we simply recognize and know, for example, that there's the possibility of an instantaneous universal holocaust; that nations are building up their stockpiles; that countries are exploding these nuclear weapons almost every month. And there is danger to the environment, danger to our lives, danger to all living things. We live under that constantly. Some people may feel the world's going off course. They have that sense of loss.

Others are sensing loss with social problems. There's hardly any one of you who doesn't know a family that's broken up; twenty, twenty-five, thirty years and they're divorced. You say, "What's happening here?" Lawyers tell me that in the old days the husband and wife used to fight terribly over the custody of the children in a divorce. There's been such a reversal that they fight over who doesn't get the children.

The whole question of crime in the streets; all these things. People suddenly say, "We've lost our moorings," and they feel that society is drifting. They have that sense of loss.

Others feel a sense of loss with their church, their church which used to be so secure, the church which used to have so many wonderful things you and I knew growing up, with the novenas, the benedictions, smoke, and incense. We had the certainties, the sureties, that all over the world these things were the same. Today we wonder. One priest says this, another priest says that. Parishes differ radically from one to another. Answers aren't so certain. We wonder if our children will have the faith that we were brought up on. People feel that the church can't get its act together, as it were. There's a sense of loss.

Others are made to have this sense of being lost—children from broken homes brought up indifferently; children who are hurt or not wanted; children whose psyches are damaged early;

children who are abused physically. We know that statistics tell us that one out of every six or seven are physically abused, not the ordinary spanking, but physical abuse to such an extent that every year sixty thousand children die from it. Abused and abandoned children certainly grow up with a sense of being lost.

There are places such as Odyssey House all over the country, to help youngsters who have family problems, running away from home, drug problems. The staff of one of these Odyssey Houses last year reported that sixty of the 144 young women in their program had been the victims of incest before they were twelve. It's something we don't hear much about, but something that's surfacing more and more, and apparently there's a lot more of this than we've ever realized. These kids are forced to have a sense of being lost and unworthy, of being bad and evil, and are made to feel totally hopeless, to have a poor self-image. People are made to feel lost in life.

And finally, of course, there is the sense of loss that comes to us adults—the stages of life, the crises of life. This hasn't been studied too much, but as you progress through your thirties, forties, fifties, and sixties, there are certain critical points, or you're suddenly confronted with something, such as a heart attack, and a whole readjustment of your life afterwards.

This occurs at certain stages of life—that middle-age crisis when the job is good, but it's not everything anymore. Or the marriage is fine, but there's something missing. The friendships, the possessions, the cocktail parties, the house—there's a gnawing emptiness, a feeling that your powers are lessening, a feeling of being over the hill, a feeling that things are slipping by, a feeling of questioning the basics of life, a feeling of coming to terms with death, a sense of your own mortality. There is a sense that all of a sudden things are shifting. It seems that science is getting a little closer to the old folklore that every seven years that itch comes. It's not the seven-year-itch of running around, but the seven-year-itch of reassessment, of feeling lost, of realigning your moorings. Sometimes there's crisis.

I was just reading Gail Sheehy's book *Passages*, about the predictable crises in adult life. Understandably, there will be crises that we'll go through after we're thirty or forty years old. In her first chapter, she tells about her own particular crisis. Here she is, thirty-five years old, mother, divorcée, journalist, prize winner, on assignments, living with a man, an enormously exciting, glamorous, and engaging life.

But all of a sudden, when she was over in Northern Ireland on a typical assignment to interview Irish women, she was talking to a young Irish lad, and in an instant, a bullet ripped through the air, and he turned his face at the wrong moment; he lost his face.

And then the shooting started, and bodies were falling on top of her. She and the others who were down in the street tried to crawl upstairs to the balconies, to hide in the houses. They finally were led in, and mothers and children were hovering as British troopers came in and were spraying the air with bullets. And she saw three teenage boys run across and be cut down like dummies in a carnival. She saw the priest waving his white handkerchief, going over to minister to the boys, cut down and killed instantly. Another man who knelt to say a prayer for them was shot dead.

In a few minutes, thirteen people lay dead. Three or four bodies had only moments before laid pressing on top of her. And all of a sudden she began to have a sense of panic and fear. She had heard about death, and seen it, but this was the first time it fell, literally, on top of her. And all of a sudden she began to waver and couldn't cope with this.

A little later she reached out to the one person who might help her—the man in New York she was living with who was in the newspaper business—and she called him and he was rather breezy as she was saying, "There's thirteen people who have just been killed here."

And he's saying, "Well, I told you, just interview the Irish women," and so forth, and she just suddenly felt terribly alone.

She says this, if I could just quote a brief section:

From the moment I hung up on that non-conversation my head went numb, my scalp shrank. Some dark switch was thrown and a series of weights came to roll across my brain. I had squandered my one wish to be saved. The world was negligent. Thirteen could perish—or thirteen thousand—I could perish—and tomorrow it would all be beside the point.

As I joined the people lying on their stomachs, a powerful idea took hold: no one is with me, no one can keep me safe, there is no one who will ever leave me alone. I had a headache for a year.

When I flew home from Ireland I couldn't write the story, couldn't confront the fact of my own mortality. In the end I dragged out some words and made the deadline, but at an ugly price. My short temper lengthened into diatribes against the people closest to me, driving away the only sources of support that might have helped me to fight my demons. I broke off with the man who had been sharing my life for four years, fired my secretary, lost my housekeeper, and found myself alone with my daughter.

As spring came I hardly knew myself. The rootlessness that had once been such a joy in my early thirties, allowing me to burst the ropes of old roles, to be reckless and selfish, and focused on stretching my new-found dream and liberation, to roam the world on assignment and then to stay up all night typing, on caffeine and nicotine—all at once that didn't work any more. Some intruder shook me by the psyche and shouted, "Take stock. Half of your life has been spent. What about the part of you that wants a home and talks about a second child?"

Before I could answer, the intruder pointed to something else I had postponed. "What about the side of you that wants to contribute to the world? Words, books, demonstrations, donations; is this enough? You have been a performer, not a full participant, and now you are thirty-five." To be confronted for the first time with the arithmetic of life was quite simply, terrifying.

She goes on to describe this crisis that all of a sudden caught her up short. The whole book is dedicated to people from her age on who meet with different crises of life that are inevitable, who have this sense of loss, of being alone. Suddenly the glamor, the job, the liberated newspaperwoman didn't matter any more. She came to a critical turning point; she felt alone; she was lost. This is the kind of thing that Paul was describing. This is the kind of thing Paul wants to get across to you and me. This is the kind of thing Paul was saying. Paul was probably in his fifties when he was converted. A successful man, all of a sudden feeling his life going by; all of a sudden something hit him; all of a sudden things he leaned on, depended on, and thought would save him, suddenly, like molasses under his feet, gave way.

As he says, "I was once a blasphemer. I was filled with arrogance. The worst of sinners." He couldn't be more lost than that. That's the first part of Paul's message. But there's a second part, of course. Paul is saying, "Not only was I lost, but I was found." That's the message of this scripture.

"And I was found," he says, "by God's unspeakable mercy in Jesus," because Paul was a contemporary of Peter and the other disciples, and in spite of himself, he too heard the parables about the lost being found. He heard them tell the story that Jesus said that God would leave ninety-nine to search for one sinner. "Could that be I?" God was like the housekeeper who would sweep the house to find one lost coin. "Could that be I?" God was the doughty, old, foolish father running after his prodigal son. "Would he run after me?"

That's what happened. Paul began to realize that God's mercy was enormous. That he was lost. That he needed not only *something* to fill his middle-age life, he needed *Someone* to fill his life. That Someone was Jesus. Remember that story about Damascus when Jesus appeared to Paul and said, "Saul, Saul, why do you persecute me?" And Paul, as he was later called, says, "Who are you?" He says, "I am the Jesus you are fighting against."

In other words, this was the Jesus Paul was struggling with, and until he surrendered to Jesus, Paul would be a lost man. In surrendering to Jesus he found himself.

Paul is like the hero in an unusual book called *The Seed and the Sower*. The book tells about a very handsome, blond, fair, blue-eyed hero, very popular, very talented, but he has a great interior suffering. The reason he has a great inner suffering is because he's carrying a great deal of guilt. He has a secret guilt because he has betrayed his dark and handicapped brother.

He stops in his world travels in the little country of Palestine. And in Palestine he visits the little city of Emmaus, where Jesus appeared, you recall, to his disciples. At Emmaus he has a vision. In that vision, all of a sudden Jesus appears, lovely, alive, and radiant. And his disciples come rushing toward him, and Jesus gathers and surrounds his disciples, but all of a sudden Jesus becomes agitated, and he looks around and he says, "One of you is missing. I know; Judas! Where is Judas?" "Here I am!" cries the hero, anguished and horrified and surprised to hear these words pour from his own lips.

And he comes out of the shadows and he falls at the feet of Jesus, and Jesus lifts him up and embraces and kisses him and says, "Oh, beloved Judas, I could never have done it without you." Leave it to a merciful Lord to find some good, even in Judas.

That's the way Paul felt. He was lost, but Jesus raised him up. He was in this crisis time, and Jesus healed him. And so Paul's message is simply telling the people he's writing to: "If I, why not you? If I have received this mercy, if I can sing my 'Amazing Grace' song, so each one of you can as you hit your crisis of life."

When suddenly things become stale, flat, and unprofitable, the sign of the Spirit is perhaps that you and I are leaning on the wrong things. And although the crises of life can be hard because we feel our powers, we feel our world, we feel our wealth slipping away from us, they are great and enormous opportunities for growth and the Spirit and the embrace of Jesus. They are opportunities to be found.

So we go back to the altar, you and I, and try to remember Paul's urgent message: "I was lost, and I was found."

Sometimes you and I are lost, but we can be found, too. And the only way to be found is to open ourselves to the mercy of God in Christ Jesus.

28

✛

Images for the End of Summer: Labor Day

As we wind down the summer and come to its very end, traditionally marked by Labor Day, I would just like to share with you a few images, nothing profound, but just to let them create in your mind a sense that, if we are open to God in the ordinary ways of life, God can speak to us and give us both lesson and invitation.

One image that sticks in my mind is from a visit a friend and I made to an ethnic neighborhood in the Pittsburgh area. We had visited one of those churches with an onion-shaped dome. We had been there with a little party, and before we boarded the van a little woman who was very old and dressed in drab, worn clothes, with the traditional handkerchief, or kerchief, around her head came up to me with a big smile, a total stranger, and she took my hands in her very old, gnarled hands, and she said in perfect English: "One, two, three, four, five, six, seven, eight, nine, ten," and she smiled at me. That was the extent of her English vocabulary, and she had said it all, right there.

I was so surprised and taken by her graciousness that I smiled back at her, gave her a little kiss, this strange woman, and boarded the van. The imagery, however, stuck with me. The imagery of a woman's simple desire to please. "See," she's saying, "I can speak at least ten English words."

Her need for approval was very unemcumbered; she wasn't embarrassed, just waiting for me to say "that's nice" or to nod, or to give her some kind of body-English to say "that's great," which indeed it was. And I thought, when I reflected on this, that in her simplicity and directness she was kind of an image of a good Christian.

I thought how often our own egotism and our own cynicism and our own distrust will not permit us to do such a thing. We don't even approach God that way. We would not think of doing what she did. The image that I caught was the image of a Christian at prayer, unembarrassed, uninhibited, direct and simple and wholesome. It's an image to think about. Do we approach God that way?

The second image came when I was in New England and a few acquaintances of mine were running one of those ten-mile mini-marathons, and I saw Fred and Bill, friends of mine, finally coming around the bend; and they were alone and they were gaming out the last few hundred yards in a kind of hand-to-hand competition. There was no one visible behind them so they had a clear field. They were running almost stride for stride. And I was very much surprised when about twenty-five yards from the finish line they grabbed hands and together they came in linked, in an intentional dead heat.

And again, the image was strong as I reflected on it later. I thought about what had happened, and about priorities and values, and Christian love. And I realized what impressed me about that little incident and the image that came across was that there is something better in life than the personal desire to win an individual trophy.

I realized something that St. Paul said, that we're members of one another. Or Jesus spoke of the vine and the branches. I knew, in fact, that I had seen an image of the divine and human love. That we don't always have to be in a relationship of competitiveness with one another. That before the finish line and the prize we can join hands and in cooperation and fraternity win the prize together.

A third image comes from the desert out in the West. We were with a little group conducted by a guide. I was munching on a sandwich when a little lizard suddenly popped out of the sand and looked at me as if to say: "What are you doing in my territory?" (and he was right). I looked back at him and took a piece of the sandwich bread, thinking he might like it, tossed it at him, and he grabbed it and disappeared into the sand, out of sight.

I asked the hike leader, "How in God's name can things like this live out here? How can they survive? There's no water, no food, and no shade from this incredible heat."

And my guide simply laughed and said, "Look, there's a whole adequate supply of all these things for the peculiar needs of these creatures. It is cool underground; the plants harbor moisture; there's a vast ecosystem at work here." And he explained it to me.

And the reflection that came after a while was this: How difficult it is for people of position and power to realize that without the resources they have in their lives, people can not only survive, but they can prosper. Try to think for a moment. There are people in the world who do not have what we have. How do people survive without their VCRs? Without cars? Without movies? How do they possibly live without television? And tap water? And indoor plumbing? And heat in the winter? And air conditioning in the summer?

We get so used to these things that we forget that people not only can survive in a different way of life, but they can prosper. And that leads us to the thought that frequently poverty brings closeness and riches bring separateness.

I called to mind a little excerpt that I had read by Henri Nouwen, the great spiritual writer and priest who went to live among the poor people in Peru. He wrote:

In Peru I lived in a parish with one hundred thousand

people, sixty percent of whom were under twenty years old. I was living with a very poor family in a new town, as they call it, really a converted desert on the outskirts of Lima.

I came to realize that being a western, northern person, you always want to do something. You always want to have a plan. You see problems and you want to change something. We have a very structured kind of thinking.

Well, when I got there, I soon realized that if I wanted to approach reality that way I might as well give up. When I walked from the church to the home which was twenty minutes up a hill over a sandy, dusty road, the children would come up to me and take me by my fingers, literally, so that I didn't have any free fingers left. They climbed all over my body, they were always around me, touching and hugging me, and kissing me, looking at me, playing with me, playing all around me. They were telling me something. They were giving me a sense of "this is the day the Lord has made, let us celebrate and be glad, let's just be aware of one another."

They were indirectly unmasking my illusion of wanting to do something big. They kept laughing and playing and telling me something about life that I didn't know. In the midst of all their misery and hunger and difficulty there was a life-giving reality. I see my life as very serious and very important and those kids were laughing at it all the time. They were playing with it as if to say "what are you worrying about? Here we are."

I had a sense of being given a lot of feeling. In fact, it blew away my depression in a way that no psychotherapist could do. They just transcended it, right away.

And those are images to think about. How can people be happy without our taken-for-granted luxuries? How can they be close? And how can children in misery laugh in Lima, Peru? And how can they play and sing when we can't do that with all that we have? How, in their situation, can they play and sing, and hold hands, and fall down on the ground and rejoice? But they can. How do they survive except through prayer and an abiding sense of community? That's a powerful image.

And the final one. Matthew's a very beautiful grandnephew of mine, a gift from God. When I was home last time, my niece saw me in the kitchen having a little bite to eat, and she said to Matthew, "Go in and give your uncle a kiss."

He had been playing in the garden. He was covered with soot, dirt, from head to toe. He ran over to me and planted a big kiss, saying, "I love you." And again, I was not only touched by the reality, but by the imagery that came. And I thought to myself, "How like that child are we. God loves us and we approach God with a grimy kiss. God looks through our messiness and our dirt, looks through all of these things that are wrong and sees, basically, innocence and a desire to love. And God is like that. God accepts our grimy kiss and is pleased with our coming to God, no matter what our condition."

So these are images for the end of the summer. An old woman counting fingers, openly needing approval, wanting to please, directly approaching another human being, reminding us that we should treat God that way.

Two runners, instead of competing to the end, joining hands in making it a mutual victory and sharing. How much like the Christian gospel that imagery is.

A hard and difficult desert, supporting enormous and colorful life in ways that we know not, to remind us that often all that we have may be a hindrance not only to God, but to one another.

And finally, a child's grimy kiss. The imagery of how God accepts us through all our dirt and messiness and is delighted that we approach, however we are.

These are images to pray about, to think about, at the end of summer. Perhaps we can even put their messages into practice.

29

✝

The Road to Emmaus

Luke 24:1–35

The road to Emmaus story is one of the great and wonderful stories that have come down to us, probably the most popular one next to the stories of the good Samaritan and the prodigal son.

But for all of its marvelousness, it is interesting to note that the biblical scholars and the archaeologists have yet to discover just where this little town of Emmaus was. They haven't quite found its location. And maybe just as well, I think, because the way the gospel is written, the road to Emmaus story is less an account of geography than it is a story of everyman's and everywoman's journey.

And it's a universal journey, a kind of prototype story of human existence itself because the simple fact is that every human being, you and I and everyone who's ever lived, is a sojourner. We're all travelers on that long-ago and ever-present road of life. All of us, therefore, as the gospel suggests, travel the same way.

Moreover, our Emmaus story has the same three elements that are common to every journey story, religious or folkloric, that is found in every culture, society, and time. The first element that is common to all is that a supernatural guide is on the road with us. You might remember the story of Tobias. The archangel Raphael was the traveler who finally cured Tobias of his blindness, but he kept his identity hidden and Tobias didn't know him as an angel—at least not till the very end of the story. Then we have all those folklore stories of kings who put on beggar's clothes and wander around their kingdoms to see how things are going. We have in our tradition the story of Martin of Tours, a catechumen, who saw a beggar on the side of the road, cut his soldier's cloak in half, and gave half to the beggar. That night he had a dream and in his dream the beggar appeared wearing half the cloak, and the beggar was Christ.

I remember an old story my mother told us kids—which I'm sure was a common story in those days—about St. Peter going about in disguise. He came to this little cottage and a woman came to the door. She was dressed in a little red cap, a white apron, and a black dress. She was baking many loaves of bread. She had hundreds of them. And Peter said, "May I have just a little morsel? I'm so hungry." And the greedy woman said, "No!" and slammed the door in his face, not knowing, of course, that it was St. Peter. And, what's more, a hot-headed St. Peter! So he pronounced a curse on her that she would forever have to search for her food. So there was a sudden explosion of smoke and when it cleared, the woman flew out of her cottage chimney as a woodpecker to eke out and peck out her living. She still wears, as you may notice, her red cap, white apron, and black dress.

We thought that story was marvelous—and scary. We certainly got the point. There are supernatural presences on the road of life, you see, like Jesus on the road to Emmaus, and they join us en route. That's the first element. It's common to all journey stories, as I've said, including our gospel.

The second element is always this: human blindness and the resulting disappointment. The human blindness is that we simply don't perceive or recognize the presence. We're walk-

ing with St. Peter, or the king, or the archangel Raphael, or
Jesus, but we don't know it. We don't recognize the divinity or
the presence. Our "eyes are held." And because we don't recognize the presence we are frequently disappointed. You can
hear that disappointment in the complaints of the two disciples as they talk to the stranger: "We had thought that we
would finally be rescued. We had hoped that this Jesus would
have been the one to set things right. It's been three days now
since they killed him and, along with him, our hopes."

And so, not knowing the divine presence that is with them,
they fall, like most people, into despair or cynicism. They echo
the age-old cry of us all, "Where is God?" And the cry is particularly poignant in times of distress, brokenness, tragedy, or
death. We had hoped that God would rescue us but God failed
and didn't rescue us. Where is God? We have no hint that God
is present or cares about what we're going through. Our eyes
are held.

The third element common to all journey stories is also
present in our road to Emmaus story, and that is revelation.
There is a certain point in the journey of human life when people recognize that they are not alone. Usually such a discovery
is made in hindsight. Like our two disciples who had the revelation of the risen Christ in the breaking of the bread. Later on,
in hindsight, on their way back to Jerusalem, they are com-
pelled to remark, "Were not our hearts burning inside us on
the road as he opened the scriptures to us?" Put in other
words, they are saying in effect, "Now that we think about it,
when we were walking along that road, complaining, being
bitterly disappointed and hurt and pouring it all out to that
stranger whom we didn't recognize at the time—wasn't there
something we couldn't put our finger on? Wasn't there a grace
there?"

And often this is the way it is with us. You think of times in
your life that were messy and difficult and hard. And think of
years later, looking back and saying, "I wouldn't want to go

through it again, but now I can see that there was a grace there. I probably would not be in the church today if it were not for this or that. It was a terrible time in my life but still—there was a divinity, a supernatural presence. God had something in mind for me. At the time I didn't understand it, I didn't recognize it, but in hindsight, I am what I am by the grace of God. God did touch me. God was there. I can see that now." Revelation, however belatedly, has taken place.

So every story goes through those three steps. First, there's a supernatural guide. Second, we don't always recognize it, which is why we are frequently disappointed and bewildered. Finally, however, in due time we come face to face with the revelation. Also—and this is critical—in every story like our road to Emmaus story, there is a point of entry. What finally brings about the recognition, the revelation? How do we break through to a sense that we are not alone, that walking with us is a God who is madly in love with us and who does care?

The Emmaus story gives us the telltale clue. In one word the clue is: hospitality. That's a synonym for what we call the spiritual and corporal works of mercy. It's the synonym for the good deed, the love that is given even when we get nothing out of it.

In our gospel story, the point of entry was that Near East urgency that a stranger should not travel alone on a dangerous road. So the two disciples insisted on hospitality, "Come, it's getting late. Share our food, share our hospitality." The revelation came precisely at that moment when they forgot themselves and their disappointments and hurts, the moment when they focused on another. The good deed, the reaching out, was their point of entry that revealed the Christ who was there all along. On their journey the presence, thus far hidden from their eyes, was revealed in the shared breaking of the bread.

Now we see why the Emmaus story is also our story. Why it is eternal and timeless. It's a story saved by the church in order to remind us and encourage us that we do not walk alone; that it is okay to be disappointed and okay to complain and okay to talk about hopes that have been dashed and okay even to wonder if anybody cares. But the story also promises us a caring presence and ultimately a revelation which, as we said, often comes in hindsight. More importantly, the Emmaus story urges us meanwhile—while we wait for things to get better—to deeds of love and charity and neighborliness, for such things, it promises, will be our point of entry to finally recognizing someday that Jesus Christ broke bread with us.

30

✝

Untie Him

John 11:1–44

This is an interesting gospel because of the final words that give us a clue to what life and death are all about. Jesus says, "Untie him," referring to Lazarus. "Let him go."

We, who so many centuries later reflect on those words, ask ourselves, "Well, we read the story and it's a very dramatic one, obviously, but does Jesus say the same words today? And if he does, how does it work?"

The answer, of course, as you suspect, is that Jesus does say those same words and he does it through a community of faith and a community of love. Let me share with you a story, a true story of a young man named Peter Finley. To appreciate his story you have to imagine yourself as nineteen years old, old enough to enjoy very vigorous life, vigorous health, the ability to love. At that age one exults in one's body and strength and powers, rejoices in one's mind and powers. At nineteen many are look-ing ahead to a successful future and a second year of college.

Well, in Peter's case this whole dream was somewhat shattered when it was discovered that he had leukemia. For three years this nineteen-year-old man suffered a terrible battle with the deadly disease. And finally, he received a bone marrow transplant, and he wrote these words which I'd like to share with you: "It seemed that I triumphed physically and spiritually over my disease, and that life in abundance was to be my reward."

Well, he was exhausted by the ordeal, of course, but strength returned slowly every day, and this gives a clue to why. It was not just because of the triumph of medicine. But listen once more to what Peter said: "I believed then that the combination of my will to live and the intense love poured forth by the members of my church and by many others have brought about a miracle and that I was finally cured."

And so in a sense, when you reflect on Peter's story, you come back to the Lazarus motif. Here was a young man dying, bound by the strong bands of leukemia, and Jesus in the community stood before him and said, "Untie him of this restrictive bond, and let him go." And it was the love of the community that enabled him to find this.

Well, the question comes for Peter and for Lazarus: What did they do with their new lives? Peter went on swimming and walking on the beach, very simple things, mostly touching the people he loved, as he said. And then looking to long-range plans to continue his college. And he thought of himself as a normal college student, but he had this insight, and again I'd like to share his words. He said, "I had learned the hard way that graduate school, a law degree, and the MCATs were not the things that truly counted in life. Returning to health, coupled with what I had learned about the importance of love, made life seem like heaven to me."

For a young man, that's a great insight. He shares his sense of priorities. He could have been bound by many cords that young people and older ones are bound by. But Jesus had stood in the community and called down the power of God and said, "Untie this young man," not only from his leukemia, that was secondary, but also from false values, so that he could truly be free.

I'd like to say that there's a happy end to the story of Peter Finley, but there's not, because the leukemia returned. And when it did after a couple of years, Peter understandably felt quite betrayed. He said he thought death was just grinning at him and making a mockery of the whole thing. But then in his despairing moments he discovered the same truth over again—that God does not cease working. And so he turned once more to his friends to share the awful news that once more he had incurred the dreaded leukemia. And he cried with them and talked with them and wanted to be sustained by them. And through that, another important change happened to him. He began to have another sense of hope. He had planned for the future, but now the future wasn't in terms of years or decades, but rather in terms of each new day. And again, he says, and I quote him: "Because I knew I was loved, and therefore would always be happy, I could ask new questions. What did I want to do with each day allotted to me?"

That's quite a journey for a young man. But in both instances Jesus stood before him in a loving community of faith and said, "Untie him and let him go."

We try to translate Peter Finley's experience of Jesus and the Lazarus story to what we know today. The metaphor of tying is very strong. There are people who are bound with all kinds of pressures, and Jesus has to stand there through you and through me and really find release for these people.

The high school proms are coming up, and the other day in the paper I saw a big ad directed to young people; it was advertising the "Miami Vice" and the "Dynasty" clothes that they can wear to the prom, which is okay, it's part of the event. The question is how many are able to see through that ad and to have enough discernment to see that the lifestyle that is being advertised is most blinding and most constricting and eventually will suffocate us to death, and the people that we touch.

You think of a young, promising man like Dwight Gooden,

the great baseball pitcher. He's in his twenties. He's a million-aire. And not too long ago he was in rehab for cocaine abuse, with a gun-toting girlfriend who left him after she found out he fathered a child with somebody else.

Look at the people in this sordid story. The baby who is born out of wedlock to some girl somewhere. The girl herself who has no husband, and the baby now has no father except a millionaire who's done time for drugs. The drug dealer him-self, or herself, who sold the cocaine to Dwight Gooden, cast-ing a shadow over a promising career and binding him up more than Peter Finley was by leukemia. There's the girlfriend walking around with a loaded gun, and Dwight Gooden him-self. And every one of these people in this scenario should cry out, or must cry out, "Let me go!" They are bound as bound could be.

Or you read in the paper about Johnny Carson's son who fa-thered a child out of wedlock; this was Carson's second son to father a child out of wedlock. Johnny himself is paying a mil-lion dollars in alimony to his second or third wife, and you think of all of the fame and then of the broken relationships. Think of the girls who have these babies. Think of the children being raised without fathers. Think of the ex-wives. Is this free-dom? They are much more bound than Peter Finley ever was. Who will release them? Who will stand before the young peo-ple of our world and say, "But this is slavery and not freedom. Let him go. Untie these people"?

Or you read about Dean Martin's son who was killed. In looking over the little news item it mentions casually that this young man in his early thirties had been married three times. Three times, three broken relationships. Three deaths, besides his own physical death. Again, people are bound. Who's going to stand before them and cry out, "Let them go, untie them"?

They're bound by their addictions, by false values, by what the media sell, by the world's concept of success, by life in the fast lane, as we call it. These are people who are our Lazaruses of today.

And then there is the great cry of those bound by poverty

and want and hunger and homelessness. They need release as much as Lazarus ever did.

The Peter Finleys of this world have the power of Jesus, and they have been untied—untied in spirit even though a Peter Finley might eventually die a physical death from leukemia. There are so many more who are bound and the only way that Jesus works is through his living community, such as you and me. And by our charity and prayer, and by our insistence on the values of the gospel. We stand before the world and we offer to untie those who are bound and to give them freedom, to let them go, to let them be themselves.

So as you listen to or read this gospel, that old and lovely story of Lazarus, maybe you can think of the Lazaruses that you know who are in the tomb. Think of the Lazarus, Dwight Gooden. Think of the Lazarus, Dean Martin's son. Think of the Lazaruses sleeping on the grates of New York City or Jersey City. Think of the Lazaruses who are addicted like Dwight Gooden. Think of the Lazaruses who sell the addictions for money. Think of the Lazaruses who use people and bind them up by greed. Think of all those Lazaruses who need release, and where will Jesus be?

There's only one answer for a believer. You and I must raise our hands to say, "Here we are. Untie him, and set him free."

31

+

Holy Thursday

John 13:1–17

A part of this reading from St. John's gospel is missing. Luke supplies it in his gospel account, and what he supplies would be comic if it weren't so tragic. The Last Supper scene is one of high drama. Jesus is leaving his dying legacy. He delivers his long soliloquy, speaking of Abba, Father, his love for his disciples, his worry that they would scatter when he was gone, his tremors of betrayal, his fears, his hopes. On Jesus goes when, in the midst of these great and noble words, in the midst of his heartfelt unburdening, an irrelevant, petty dispute arises among his disciples. "Who is the greatest among them?" they want to know!

It reminds me of a time some years ago when I was giving a long lecture on the deep theology of ministry and parish, plumbing the scriptural and doctrinal depths with, I thought, learned explanations and expositions. After an hour I was through, and like a good lecturer I asked if there were any questions. This gentleman raised his hand and asked, "Is the parish ever going to have racks for bikes?" For the first time in my life I was speechless. I just couldn't reverse gears fast enough to answer him.

It reminded me of the old hunting story of the deer hound which set off one morning chasing a magnificent buck. A few minutes into the chase a fox crossed the path and the hound veered off to chase the fox. A little later a rabbit crossed that path and the hound was soon baying after the rabbit. Then a squirrel crossed the path and the dog was soon pounding after him. Finally, a field mouse crossed the path and the hound chased it into its burrow. The deer hound had begun chasing a great buck and wound up watching a mousehole.

Well, I wonder, when the disciples broke in with their irrelevancy, what was Jesus' reaction? Did he roll his eyes and shake his head? Did he weep? Did he laugh because ultimately he saw the humor of it? Anyway, what he did do was to figure that maybe, after all, the disciples' nonsense might give him a way to get his teachings and feelings across, and so in a way he responded to their distraction by saying in effect, "Watch this." So he got up and grabbed something. Now we must remember that in his society Jesus was a layman. He was not a cleric, not a priest. And so the holy garment he put on was not an elegant robe or vestment, but a towel. Then he next took a pitcher and basin of water and began to wash his disciples' feet.

When he came to Peter, Peter, as we know, protested. This was because Peter, being the leader and likely the sharpest of the disciples, saw the implications. He reacted much like we also would have reacted and do react. We instinctively shrink from this sort of thing. I mean, *we* can be humble before God, but not the other way around. Think of the embarrassment of having a visiting dignitary come to your house for dinner. He asks to use the bathroom and while there sees a spot on the floor and you discover him on his knees cleaning your bathroom floor. Never mind that you cleaned the bathroom floor for him, but that *he* should do it for you—it's too much, too overwhelmingly embarrassing.

It is worth remembering that John has no mention of the institution of the eucharist in his gospel. By the time he wrote this last of the four gospels the eucharist was taken for granted. So he gives us an interpretation of what the eucharist means, and he does that through the scene of the washing of the feet. Both using simple bread and washing feet become interchangeable symbols of what Jesus was about, and again, once more, the implications are there.

I mean, we want God in all God's glory, goodness and greatness. We want God in all God's majesty, power, and transcendence. We can handle that—God's remoteness. But for God to wash our feet, to put on a towel rather than a robe, to be simple bread, to be that close is embarrassing—and frightening.

Frightening for two reasons. First, we are confronted with the question that his actions forced. Is God like *that*? Not in heaven, but on this earth washing feet? Second, this is frightening because when it was all done with, this dreadful and mortifying act, Jesus gave a mandate. Now the word "mandate" comes from the Latin *mandatum*, from which we get the English word "Maundy," which is why we call this day "Maundy Thursday"—the day the mandate was given to serve, to break bread, and *therefore* to reveal the presence of Christ. No wonder Peter blanched and protested the implications! No wonder we do. Every time we meet to break the one bread and share the one cup, the *mandatum*, the mandate, is there.

This, very simply, is what our eucharist is about, our Mass. The presence of the almighty in basic bread and the mandate to be bread to others. To break open the word of scripture, to consecrate bread and wine and so bring Christ among us become both our comfort and our challenge.

This is what we celebrate on Holy Thursday. The gift of God, but what a God! The gift of a God who gives his flesh and blood and with no apology leaves us with the mandate to do the same.

32

+

Easter

John 20:1–18

Stories about golfers' fanaticism are legendary. Here's one to add to your repertoire. A golfer named George finally got home. "George," his wife scolded, "you promised you'd be home at four o'clock. Look, here it is eight o'clock." George protests, "But, honey, please listen to me. Poor old Fred is dead. He just dropped over right there on the eighth green." "Oh, that's terrible," his wife exclaimed. "It surely was," said George. "For the rest of the game it was hit the ball, drag Fred, hit the ball, drag Fred."

Well, the laughter is good for two reasons. One is reflected in the custom in some parts of Eastern Catholicism to tell jokes on Easter Sunday to imitate God's last laugh on Satan, who thought he had won with the death of Jesus. The other reason is that it may be the last laugh you get from this homily because my message may prove disturbing and annoying to some. My message is that Easter, as we know it, is a fraud.

What do we associate with Easter? Easter bunnies, Easter eggs, crocuses blooming, hyacinths and tulips as gifts to Mom, springtime, the first robin, cocoons soon to bring forth butterflies. Ah, yes, the sweet resurrection of nature is all around us.

And we say that Jesus is like that, a variation of spring. We liken him to the lowly caterpillar who was wrapped in the cocoon of death on Calvary and on Easter Sunday emerged as a divine butterfly and went his way to sit at the right hand of God in heaven. A lovely springtime tableau but, of course, it's all pure parody, pure pagan drivel.

Easter is *not* bunnies and butterflies. Easter is about a body that somehow got loose. It's about a dead Jesus, horribly crucified, who came back to harass us. And that scares the hell out of us. Easter is about a Jesus who while alive was so radical, so countercultural that the prevailing culture killed him. He was a threat to the world as it was and is more of a threat now that he's footloose after the resurrection. Bunnies and butterflies we can handle, but a risen Christ, just as radical as he ever was, is too much. Maybe that's why we settle for spiritual Disneyland.

But the plain fact is that Jesus is not Disneyland. He is a way of life. He is not Dear Abby or Leo Buscaglia or, God forbid, Dr. Ruth dispensing advice and warm fuzzies and what we want to hear. He is demand. He is not flow, he is counterflow, counterculture, because the culture is wrong and selfish and sinful as it is. If you don't believe me, remember that this is the culture that gave us Hiroshima, Dachau, and Auschwitz; racism, discrimination, poverty in the midst of plenty, drugs that crossfire young lives into oblivion, and a Savings and Loan scandal so riddled with fraud that every American will pay for decades to come. To see just how much Jesus is opposite to these things, how countercultural Jesus is and the Christianity he founded is, look at life from the bottom up, from the other side.

Take a sensitive issue. Jesus speaks of no divorce and would not be swayed by jargon about "an exciting new option for personal freedom." Looked at from the bottom up, divorce is a painful tragedy; it is parents abandoning their children. Period. And that brutal fact hurts and continues to hurt as every study ever produced shows.

A very recent survey by *Seventeen* magazine shows that 24 percent of fifteen year olds have had sex. By age eighteen that figure climbs to 60 percent. From the bottom up view, the annual one and a half million babies being aborted are the most unfree in a free-sex culture. All over America parents who already have raised *their* families are newly bound in raising the second families of their teenage children. And those dying slowly from AIDS would like to take a second look, if they had the time, at the promises of the sexual revolution.

Don Mattingly of the New York Yankees just signed for nineteen million dollars—nineteen million dollars!—to play baseball while the poor in squalid Brazilian barrios or the homeless of New Jersey haven't even nineteen dollars or nineteen cents. Jesus weeps over that. The self-centered twenty-five-year-old adolescents who, as the newscasts show us, pay seven thousand dollars to have hyped-up stereos in their cars, who have that kind of disposable income to disturb neighborhoods and spend on themselves and their empty lives without a thought to the needy, they are very much a part of a culture that should find Jesus Christ disturbing—because he would find *them* disturbing.

The glitter and glitz of Atlantic City's multimillion dollar casinos stand in mock contrast to the squalor and poverty just a few streets away. The minority and elderly poor of that city are still waiting for some trickle of the millions spent each day in their city. Would Jesus go to Atlantic City? Not on your life. Unless it were to sit in the middle of the road with a half-fed child between his knees, midway between the casinos and squalor in silent witness until they carted him away for disturbing the peace. Unless it were to show Donald Trump a better way or to remind him and Ivana that they have three children who have a far more desperate need for parents than for publicity.

At this point, you say, hold it! Let's go back to some more golfers' jokes. A little lightness, please. At least bring in some bunnies and butterflies. After all it's Easter and I have my parents and children here and we want to hear something nice. It's part of the holiday.

But I tell you, I would like to say something soft and innocuous about Easter—but the fact is, it's not there. What *is* there is

a Jesus who said that it's easier for a camel to pass through an
eye of a needle than for a rich person to enter the Kingdom. He
said it. I didn't. He said to seek first the Kingdom of God,
which he described as feeding the hungry and giving drink to
the thirsty. In short, being concerned about others. He told
those disturbing stories about the rich man and Lazarus at the
gate; about the man who built bigger and bigger barns—
security annuities—only to die that night without having
kissed his children.

He spoke about forgiving one's enemies as a condition for
being forgiven ourselves, for being whole. He said that. I
didn't. He said that we do not live by bread alone. He asked:
What does it profit us if we gain the whole world and lose our
very souls? He spoke of treating women with respect and not
even lusting after them in one's heart. He said nothing about
safe sex. He spoke of compassion and he gave everyone he met
a second chance. He said that we were to absolutely and without equivocation believe in God and God's wild, wild love for
us and that we count far more than the sparrow that falls to
the ground.

And what's more—and this is the clincher for which he was
killed by the culture—he actually *did* those things! He fed the
poor and healed the sick and took time with friends and
prayed and threw out money-changers, hugged children, and
had little patience with hypocrites, religious or otherwise. Oh,
he was countercultural all right. His choice. His values. You
can see that, in the long run, his culture could do nothing but
pin him to a cross. And so they did.

But what a revolting development occurred, as television's
Chester A. Riley used to say. Jesus' Abba—the "daddy" he
spoke so much of—turns right around and sets him free and
he's at his mischief again! What are we to do? We've run out of
crosses to nail him to, so we go one better. We make him over
into our image so we can go on living our lives and being very
much a part of our culture so that no one knows we're Christian. As for Jesus, we drag him out for baptisms and first com-
munions—so sweet—and Christmas, Easter, and funerals. For

the rest of our lives, it's hit the ball, drag Jesus. Hit the ball, drag Jesus.

But that's not what he's all about. He's about happiness and a way of life. He's about the decisions we make at business and school. He's about honesty and caring and concern for others. He's about whistle-blowing and ethics. He's about chastity and fidelity. He's about truth. He's about making relationships work. He's about keeping one's word. He's about life—life here and hereafter for those who listen to him. He is about real joy and fulfillment. He is about a thirtyfold and a sixtyfold and a hundredfold abundance for those who are true disciples.

Jesus is radical, countercultural—and risen! He's a body got loose. *That's* the Easter message. He has nothing against caterpillars, eggs, and butterflies: they belong to Hallmark. He's looking for fellow radicals. They belong to him.

33

+

A Wedding Homily:
For Kerry and David Saalfrank

1 Corinthians 13; John 15:9–17

Outside it's just begun to rain, and I suppose I ought to tell you that my eighty-three-year-old Italian mother says that in her country the wisdom is that if it rains on your wedding day, there will be no tears in the marriage—or is it the other way around?...Anyway, it's always worth listening to the wisdom of the ages, particularly the wisdom contained in the scriptures Kerry and David have chosen.

This is the wisdom that separates, as Paul does, for example, the fictions of love from the truths of love. This is the strong wisdom of Jesus, who commands that we are to love one another *as* he has loved us. And if you want to understand that "as" and how far it will go, look to the cross.

So there are wisdoms here in the scriptures and wisdoms I have learned as a professional bachelor over the years—three bits of wisdom in fact—that I would like to share with Kerry and David and all of you who are married or who may be someday.

The first is one you've heard before. It says that *life is what happens to you while you're making other plans.* So for example, Kerry and David, like all young couples, are looking forward to their dream house. It will be, of course, by the sea, with a pool, rose garden, a picket fence, and they'll have two darling, intelligent children. Well, the dream house turns out to be a cold water flat in Camden, New Jersey; the pool turns out to be a leaky cellar; the rose garden is a window box; the picket fence is a falling-down old chain-link affair; and the two darling, intelligent children turn out to be homely, rope-haired youngsters who aren't too bright at that. Whom do you blame? Whom do you complain to? Whom do you go on strike against?

Well, the immature react by running around with their hands clapped to their foreheads declaring loudly for all the world to hear that life in general and marriage in particular are unfair, a fraud. The mature, on the other hand, merely ask: What did we expect? After all, life is what happens to you while you're making other plans. And when you accept that, you accept life with all that it has to offer, the good and the bad, and in the process, you wind up accepting one another. In a word, you adjust the dream to reality, the reality of life and one another and begin to carry one another's burdens and in that process of life happening—without your realizing it—love happens.

Let me share with you a story of a very famous philosopher of a few centuries ago, a man named Moses Mendelssohn. He was brilliant, compassionate, intelligent, but he had one flaw: he was hunchbacked. Still, hunchback that he was, he fell in love with a girl named Gretchen, the daughter of a prosperous banker. Several months after he had met Gretchen, Mendelssohn visited her father and, as was the custom of the time, asked him very cautiously how he might feel about his courting his daughter. "Please," said Mendelssohn, "tell me the truth."

The father hesitated, hemmed and hawed, and then replied, "The truth, Moses, is, well, you're a fine fellow and all that but... I mean, you're very intelligent but..." And Mendelssohn finished the sentence for him. "But I am a hunchback." "Yes," said the father slowly. "I'm sorry. Any union is not possible because you are a hunchback." Mendelssohn paused and after some silence he asked, "May I at least visit her to say good-bye?" "By all means," said the father.

Mendelssohn went upstairs where Gretchen was sitting on the couch busy with needlework. She avoided looking at him and Mendelssohn eventually turned the conversation to that of marriage. In the course of the exchange Gretchen asked, "Moses, do you believe in that old saying that marriages are made in heaven?" "Oh, yes," answered Moses, "and while we're on that subject I might tell you that we have an ancient tradition that says that when a boy baby is about to be born, the angels blow trumpets to get heaven's attention and then announce to all the name of his future wife."

He went on: "So when I was about to be born the angels blew the trumpets and then announced the name of my future wife. Then they put down their trumpets, lowered their heads, and added, 'But alas, alas, she will be hunchbacked!' Then I stood up before the court of heaven and cried, 'Please, no! A girl should be fair and well formed. She will be the butt of cruel jokes. No one will want to marry her. Please, Master of the Universe, give the humpback to me and let her be well formed.' And God heard my prayer. And you know what, Gretchen? I was that boy and you are that girl."

Gretchen was deeply moved. She married Moses Mendelssohn and they had a very happy marriage.

Life is what happens to you when you're making other plans.

The second bit of wisdom I would share is this: *Even a stopped clock is right twice a day.* That means that even though every bride and groom tell each other that they are Mr. and Mrs. Perfect, reality soon sets in to tell them otherwise. I sense this change when I meet the bride and groom a year or two after the wedding. We chat about this and that and I get around to asking them how the marriage is going and they say fine and all that. And all the while I'm waiting for that little word which always and finally comes.

"*But*...." "But" meaning that they have discovered some minor and maybe a major flaw here and there. But this is the dream phase of their lives and so one or the other will declare, "Oh, yes, he or she has this or that fault, but give me enough time and I will change my partner." Translation: give me enough time to work on him or her and I will make my spouse perfect—as I am perfect. (If you want the unsettling implications of this ask yourself, "How would you like to be married to you?")

This "I will change my partner to be like me" is, of course, basically an immature kind of self-centered love. It's a far cry from the truly mature love of the couple who, say, have been married twenty-five or thirty years. This is the husband who props himself up in the marriage bed, looks down at his sleeping wife, and says to himself, "Well, there she is. She still can't cook like my mother. She's still not the world's greatest housekeeper. She still has the strangest relatives this side of the zoo. In spite of Miss Clairol, the gray is showing through and there are crow's feet around the eyes—but I love her."

She looks down at her sleeping husband and says to herself, "Well, there *he* is. Sometimes he drinks more than he should. Sometimes he stays out more than he should. He too has the strangest relatives this side of the zoo. In proportion as he's getting thinner on top he's getting thicker around the middle. But I love him."

You see they have gone all the way from "I will change my partner" to "I have accepted my partner." This is a mature love because it's the kind of love that God has for you and for me. God loves me, not as I'd like to be; not as God would like me to be. But as I am. It takes a long time to arrive at that, that is, to discover the other's limitations, but in the long run also to discover and embrace that even a stopped clock is right twice a day.

The third and final bit of wisdom concerns the family and friends of Kerry and David. It goes like this: *A friend is someone*

who knows the song in your heart and sings it back to you when you
forget how it goes.

The best couple, the most loving couple sometime or other
forget the words of love and commitment that come so easily
on a wedding day. The first seven years are usually the most
forgetful times, the critical times of amnesia. But it's up to you,
the friends of David and Kerry, by your humor, your example,
your prayers, and your own marriages, to sing into their ears
the words when they forget them. And when David and Kerry
do remember because you have reminded them, then, in the
decades to come, they will in turn sing to others. They will be
the song others can live by.

Years ago I was in another parish just north of here. And I
was there when they were building scores of garden apart-
ments, the forerunners of our coast-to-coast condos of today.
Well, there used to be a superintendent of one of those com-
plexes who could only be described as a character. A delightful, boisterous character.

He used to tell me about the original odd couple who were
among his tenants. The husband was about eighty-six and the
wife about eighty-three. They would get up late every morning, and then eventually they would leave the apartment holding hands on the way to the market, get their little groceries,
and sit on the the bench in front of the apartment. And this
used to delight the superintendent, and he had a great time
mimicking them. One day I happened to be over there just as
this couple came around the corner back from shopping, and
they were, as usual, holding hands. The superintendent saw
them, turned to me, clasped his hand to his head, and, in a
stage whisper you could hear all over town, he said, "I know
what it is about that couple. They're in love!"

Well, I knew that couple. I knew they had buried some of
their children. I knew that in their eighties they could still elec-
trify each other across a crowded room. I knew they had suffered much, but I knew too that their lives had become one.
They were lovers. They were words writ large and a song sung
strong.

I tell you this because, as I said, you are the friends of Kerry and David and you must keep singing the song of love and never permit them to forget the words. Then someday—when old and decrepit Mr. and Mrs. Saalfrank are hobbling around some old garden apartment holding hands and making ancient eyes at each other—some inspired superintendent is going to stand up on behalf of the whole human race and make the only proclamation worth making about any married couple: "I know what it is about this couple. They're in love!"

34

+

A Funeral Homily

Mark 16:1–8

Not too long ago a Soviet satellite with an atomic reactor aboard got into trouble and disintegrated over Canada, then fell to earth. I remember the fears of both the Soviets and the North Americans because of panic and because of the danger to health.

Reading about that sort of thing reminds us that not too far underneath the surface all of us live with a great deal of fear. The fear of atomic hardware falling out of the sky. And the everyday fears: the fear of losing our jobs; the fear of losing our health; the fear of losing our life's savings; the fear of another war; the fear of accidents; the fear of misfortune coming to our husbands, our wives, our parents, our children; the fear of being rejected, being unwanted; the fear of some people, as they move into old age, of being left alone without friends or family or loved ones.

And finally, of course, there is the fear of loss: the loss of our faculties, the loss of our hearing, the loss of our mobility through arthritis, the loss of our sanity, the loss of our loved ones, and the loss that we call death. Even after we suffer these losses, particularly the loss of death, then there are other fears that creep in, fears we don't always express: the fear of losing control. Why couldn't I have saved this one or that one? Why couldn't I have done more? The fear of coming to terms with our feelings of anger, like holy Job had against God.

If there is a God, why can't that God prevent babies from dying, or people from having cancer, or war or pestilence or hunger or famine, and all the other ills we suffer? We want to shake our fist at God and say, "Well, it was all right until it hit home." We're afraid to yell and scream and get terribly annoyed with God.

And then sometimes after that there's a fear of a weak faith. "What kind of faith do I have? It's all right when I talk to others, but when it hits home, can I come to terms with all of these realities?"

It is all these kinds of fears that like so many mountains fall upon us, and like the people in our gospel, faced with the huge, great stone covering the tomb, they say, "Who's going to lift the stone?" God says, "I will."

Because from the fear of being unwanted or unloved, from the fear of death and all its anxieties, from the fear that there's no more to life than a bunch of molecules and ashes left over, God says through the prophets, "Tell the people: 'Behold, I have loved them with an everlasting love.'" And through Isaiah the prophet, God says, "Tell the people: 'Is it possible for a mother to forget the child of her womb? And even if it were possible that a mother could forget her own child, I shall not forget thee.'"

So it is God who is the one who will lift our fears, and we must believe in that.

One of the greatest teachers of this century was the great philosopher and theologian Karl Barth; and in his old age, as people are wont to do, someone asked him what was the most important truth that he had learned in all of his vast study and thinking. And Karl Barth answered by quoting that old Protestant hymn that he learned in childhood. He said, "It's all in these words: 'Jesus loves me, this I know.'" And that was the conviction of decades of learning and studying; and he believed that.

You see the whole point of faith is that when we are met with this fear of darkness and death, we are not ashamed to call out, because the whole point of believing is the conviction that there is someone there to answer. It's what you parents have experienced when your children were very small and the lights went out at night and they got scared—those little back-up night lights were all right, but they were a short-term solution. The only way the children's fears could possibly be allayed was for mommy and daddy to go in and soothe the children, and pat them on the head, and soothe away the bad dreams, and tuck them in bed all over again, and give them those famous centuries-old words of reassurance, "Now, now, it's all right, it's all right." And the secret of allaying those fears is, of course, love. It is the love of the mother and the love of the father that eventually still the children's worst anxieties, and put them back into that sleep of innocent peace.

It's the same way with us: when we are faced with this great anxiety called death, we don't know whether to run the whole gamut of acceptance to anger, to disbelief, to hurt, to bewilderment, because after all, in death we always lose a person. But we have to remember that we never lose our relationship to God. We still have someone who says, "It's all right." That someone is God: God present in his word, in the Spirit, and in the church. And it is in all these ways that God pats us on the head, and tucks us back into bed, and says, "Even though you have fears and anxieties, it's all right."

Jesus made it all right, because it's this kind of love that burst the bonds of death. It is the kind of love that Jesus had that simply took away death's final word and made God's comfort the final word—instead of the grave. And this is what we must believe. Jesus said in the gospel, "Do not fear, little flock. It has pleased the Father to give you the Kingdom."

That's what we celebrate at a liturgy like this. Many of you are old hands at liturgies like this. You know well enough why we sing "Alleluia" as we enter the church. We sing that "Alleluia" because through our tears we believe that God has made it "all right" for the person who has died.

We wear the white vestments and put out gay flowers, not because we're insensitive to human grief, but it's our limited way of saying, "Now, now, it will be all right."

We cover the dark coffin with the white cloth of the dead person's baptismal innocence because that's the way of saying, "It's all right."

We bring the body and put it in front of the baptismal font beneath the crucified Savior because John says that out of Jesus' side flowed that blood and water with which we have been renewed. And that's our way of saying, "It's all right."

And finally, we're at this Mass where bread shall be taken, and wine brought up and changed into the body and blood of Christ, and broken and crushed and given, because today Jesus is still saying, "This is my body given for you. This is my blood shed for you—and for the one who has died."

And this, above all, is our greatest assurance that God pats us on the head and says, "It's all right."

So we go back to the altar with that double stream of feeling: human grief and loss, especially having known someone who suffered a long time. A sense of relief that it's all over because it's been a long, hard road for everybody. A sense of bewilderment, facing death so squarely and closely. But above all, I hope, a sense of faith. Faith that God gives us in our collective selves and this ancient liturgy. And faith in the promises that God made, the pat on the head, the allaying of our fears, the uplifting of our hopes, the forgiveness of our anger, the strengthening of our faith, and the promise that through Jesus, as our liturgy says, life is never ended but merely exchanged. And so for Robert, as for us, "it's all right."

35

✝

A Funeral Homily: A Young Suicide

Luke 7:11–17

As I look out over this congregation brought here by the common bond of the tragic death of someone we knew, I know that words are inadequate to temper our grief. Therefore, I shall try to make my words brief and address them to three groups of people. The first words concern John; the second concern John's friends and peers and classmates who are here—to the great credit of your friendship and sympathy for his family—in great numbers; and the third concern all of us, but especially John's family.

As for John, I presume that no one here is unaware that he took his own life. I think we ought to say that out loud so that we can hear it publicly and not just whisper this open secret among ourselves, and so that we can try to deal with it. But I want to share with you that often this deed, in the confused mind of a troubled person, is done out of love. A misguided and wrong-headed love, but love nevertheless.

The thinking of a person who is deeply troubled frequently goes like this: I am a burden. I'm hurting people. I'm in the way. I'm making a mess of things. I'm unhappy and making others unhappy. I worry those nearest to me. It would be kinder for everyone if I took the burden off their shoulders, if I weren't here, if I ceased to be. That's the understandable but backwards logic that often is at work in a person so troubled he or she doesn't see or think clearly.

And that's at least good to know. It's at least good to know that, as painful as suicide is for us, at bottom there is the truth that it is often done out of love and concern for others. It's not good thinking, but bad thinking that nevertheless has its roots in charity, not malice. And we ought to remember that about John. His tender love, as he understood it, did him in.

As for you young people here in such great numbers, John's friends and companions: for you John's death raises a question. It is this. What are you going to do about your friend's death? I mean, after the pain and the shock, after the anger—maybe at John himself, probably at God—after the hurt and tears, what are you going to do about your friend's death? It's easy to cry in his memory. What are you going to do with your life in his memory when your tears have dried?

I want to share with you a story an uncle of mine, dead himself many years now, told me because he had been there. It might suggest an answer. He told me the story of Puccini, the great Italian writer of such classic operas as *Madame Butterfly* and *La Bohème*. It seems when Puccini was fairly young he contracted cancer, and so he decided to spend his last days writing his final opera, *Turandot*, which is one of his most polished pieces. When his friends and disciples would say to him, "You are ailing, take it easy and rest," he would always respond, "I'm going to do as much as I can on my great masterwork and it's up to you, my friends, to finish it if I don't." Well, Puccini died before the opera was completed.

Now his friends had a choice. They could forever mourn their friend and return to life as usual—or they could build on his melody and complete what he started. They chose the latter. And so, in 1926—my uncle was there—at the famous La Scala Opera House in Milan, Italy, Puccini's opera was played for the first time, conducted by the famed conductor Arturo Toscanini. And when it came to the part in the opera where the master had stopped because he died, Toscanini stopped everything, turned around with eyes welling up with tears, and said to the large audience, "This is where the master ends." And he wept. But then, after a few moments, he lifted up his head, smiled broadly, and said, "And this is where his friends began." And he finished the opera.

You see the point—and the point of the question I asked you: What are you going to do about John's death? What are you going to do about his unfinished masterpiece? Will it be, in a month or so, life as usual? Or can you build on his humor, his ability, his fun, his unrealized dreams? I would suggest that if there is any fitting response to the shock of your friend's death it is life, your life, a life that's lived better, a life lived more selflessly, a life that makes a difference, a life that is honest and decent, a life that makes beautiful music for John and for the Lord. Across the chasm of death you can make John live. The music doesn't have to stop here today and doesn't have to be buried with John. You have your choice.

Finally, to all of you, to all of us, but especially to John's family, in this sad moment I leave you with an image of hope, of perspective. Picture yourselves standing on a dock beside one of those great old-time sailing vessels. It's standing there, sails folded, waiting for the wind. Suddenly a breeze comes up. When the captain senses the breeze as a forerunner of the necessary wind, he quickly orders the sails to be let down and sure enough the wind comes, catches the sails full force, and carries the ship away from the dock where you are standing.

Inevitably you or someone on that dock is bound to say, "Well, there she goes!" And from our point of view it indeed does go. Soon the mighty ship, laden with its crew and goods, is on the horizon where water and sky meet and it looks like a speck before it disappears. It's still mighty and grand, still filled with life and goods, but it's left us. We're standing on the dock quite alone. But, on the other side of the ocean, people are standing in anticipation, and as that speck on the horizon becomes larger and larger they begin to cry something different. They are crying with joy, not abandonment, "Here she comes!" And at the landing there is welcome, joy, embracing, and celebration.

We miss John. He is quickly receding from our sight, and this funeral and his burial at the cemetery are our farewells, our versions of "There he goes." But goes where? From our sight, from our embrace, from our care and love and friendship. How we miss that, how we will miss him! But he is not diminished, nor made poorer. We must remember on faith that "Here he comes!" is the cry on the eternal shore where Jesus, who understands the human heart even when it goes wrong, is waiting. And there is John, now forever larger than life, filled with life, intoxicated with life and laughter and in the arms of the One who makes all things new again, the One who says, "Welcome, John. Welcome home."

Lectionary References

1. Be Open

Mark 7:31–37, Cycle B, 23rd Sunday of the Year

2. Ananias:
   The Missing Ingredient

Acts 9:1–20, Friday of the 3rd Week of Easter

3. Bartimaeus

Mark 10:46–52, Cycle B, 30th Sunday of the Year

4. The Prodigal Son

Luke 15:11–32, Cycle C, 4th Sunday of Lent

5. Zacchaeus

Luke 19:1–10, 31st Sunday of the Year

6. Naaman:
   A Different Way

2 Kings 5:1–26, Cycle A, 28th Sunday of the Year

7. John:
   The Disquieting Prophet

Matthew 3:1–12, Cycle A, 2nd Sunday of Advent

8. Pride as Hypocrisy

Matthew 23:1–12, Cycle A, 31st Sunday of the Year

9. Capital Sins

Luke 19:45–48, Cycle C, 3rd Sunday of Lent

10. Weeds and Wheat

Matthew 13:24–30, Cycle A, 16th Sunday of the Year